the british beach guide

the british beach guide

Collected Perspectives from around the Coast

Ian Brighouse

Whittles Publishing

Published by
Whittles Publishing Ltd,
Dunbeath,
Caithness, KW6 6EG,
Scotland, UK

www.whittlespublishing.com

Printed in the UK by Severn, Gloucester on responsibly sourced paper

text and photographs © 2023 Ian Brighouse

ISBN 978-184995-555-3

for Stef

Contents

Acknowledgements

I am grateful to those who have been interviewed for this series. Thank you for your generosity of spirit and for joining in.

I owe a great debt of gratitude to Brian Banks for his skill and support.

Thank you to all my supporters, whose patronage has facilitated my "Journeys around the Coast" and enabled me to cover the whole of these wonderful islands.

Thank you to the team at Whittles Publishing for taking on the project and bringing the concept to fruition. It has been a great pleasure to work together.

Note

This volume constitutes the first collection of the beaches I have visited and is not intended as a complete guide to UK beaches. If you would like to get in touch, give feedback or add your answer to "What does the beach mean to you?" please do so via manonabeach.com/contact.

Introduction

In September 2011 I stepped onto a beach in Cornwall, where I live, and asked a stranger "What does the beach mean to you?" I filmed his answer, along with a scene-setting film and photos for context.

I had noticed that people are generally happier on the beach, and I wanted to find out why. Every day for the next year I visited a beach in Cornwall, usually early in the morning and started to collect answers. I was surprised on two counts. Firstly, why were people so open and forthcoming? We had never met and none of the interviews were pre-arranged, yet the answers came thick and fast. Secondly, the range of answers was as diverse as the moods of the sea. The beach clearly inspires creativity and connections with nature. It can be a place of reflection, work or activities and above all else, the beach uplifts us.

From all around the coast, from the remote wildness of Cullykhan in Aberdeenshire to the bustling working harbour at St Ives in Cornwall, from the vast empty sands of North Norfolk to Anthony Gormley's iron men at Crosby beach on Merseyside, I have asked people "What does the beach mean to you?"

This guide features one hundred and thirty of Britain's beaches, a cross-section of the journey so far. For each beach there is a summary, including my own impressions, plus answers from people encountered on that beach and photos. As well as being a showcase for the fine words of those who have so generously shared their answers, this is a celebration of us as an island people and an acclamation of the beach itself, this unique place where the land, sky and sea meet.

Cornwall

Summerleaze

 Parking available

 Toilets available

 Suffolk Coast Path

 Site of Special Scientific Interest

 Dogs allowed (check locally)

 RNLI Lifeguard Cover (check locally)

 Beach cleaned regularly

Good water quality

Scan me

> **"** The beach is very important, which is why I have never moved away. I come here every day and the people you meet are wonderful. Through my life it means romances, family picnics, learning to swim, Youth Club and the Sea Pool, lots of memories. **"**

1

Summerleaze is one of eight beaches in Bude, a town on Cornwall's wild Atlantic coast. Bude is hospitable and welcomes visitors, yet it remains proudly independent. The depth of affection for Bude, plus the pride of belonging to the community is palpable around town. One highlight is the tidal sea pool, which offers safe swimming. Bude also has one of only two sea locks in the country, allowing fishing boats into the safety of the inner harbour for winter. With its own cafe, the beach is flat and expansive, making it a popular place to walk dogs and exercise horses. At low tide, Summerleaze beach is an enormous expanse of sand, rock and river channel. It sits head on to the Atlantic, wild and hypnotic when you are down on the waterline.

"To be honest, the beach means everything to me. Born and bred in Bude, it's in my blood. My work as a lifeguard has passed from my father through me to my son. After fifty-five years, I'm still getting sand between my toes. The way of life means so much to me."

"It's a balm to the soul."

Trebarwith Strand

 Parking available

 Toilets available

 Suffolk Coast Path

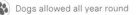 Dogs allowed all year round

 RNLI Lifeguard Cover (check locally)

 Beach cleaned regularly

 Good water quality

Scan me

> "I find the beach very inspiring to my faith, the depth of the sea and the power of it. For me, there's a beauty to it, with the very different moods of the sea at different times of the year and through the day."

At high tide there is a clash of sea and rock at Trebarwith Strand. The beach sits in a breathtakingly beautiful cove just round from Tintagel. On my first visit, clean Atlantic breakers rolled relentlessly against the black rock, the white spray framed in a bright blue sky. Time stood still. It was a mesmerising experience and I recall the shared wonder on interviewee Pippa's face. Although it is a fine, flat, sandy beach at low tide, try to get here at high tide to see what I mean. When you arrive, you will find parking and other facilities, as well as a shop and a pub that looks down on the beach from the rocky headland to one side.

> "Oh, it's fantastic. I've been coming here since childhood, visiting in the summer. This is my first visit in November. I could stand here for hours watching this. When the tide goes out, you can walk all the way along. It's a great beach for surfing too."

5

Polzeath

 Parking available

 Toilets available

 Suffolk Coast Path

 Dogs allowed (check locally)

 RNLI Lifeguard Cover (check locally)

 Beach cleaned regularly

Good water quality

Scan me

> "When we come down the following year, it's as if we have never been away. The intervening months fade into the background and we are back where we belong."

"Lots of us live in cities nowadays and it's nice to have freedom and nothing on the horizon."

Polzeath is a popular Cornish tourist destination, which claims to have the best surf in the county. The village has bars, restaurants, shops, a church and cafes next to the beach, where you can also park. At low tide there are acres of space, with nooks and crannies to hide away from the crowds, plus fine views over the sea to Pentire and Stepper Point. There's a wonderful coastal walk from Polzeath along Greenaway to Daymer Bay, celebrated by the poet John Betjeman, who is buried behind that beach at St Enedoc. The view from the higher ground at New Polzeath affords a glimpse of Greenaway, The Doom Bar and the Camel Estuary. This beach pulls visitors back every year.

"It's full of memories, happy memories with the family and with my husband. It's the highlight of the year. When we go back, I think 'We must keep this holiday spirit with us and I must spend more time with my husband and the children'."

Rock

 Parking available

 Toilets available

 Suffolk Coast Path

 Site of Special Scientific Interest

 Dogs allowed all year round

Good water quality

Scan me

"I just like to be near water. I've always enjoyed being by the sea."

Rock is a jewel in the North Cornwall crown. Sitting across the River Camel from popular Padstow, there's a serene calm in the morning here before the upmarket eateries and shops open. The beach by the river is backed by sand dunes, interlaced with intricate pathways. The views from the beach are breathtaking, all the way past Brae Hill to Daymer Bay beyond. At dawn, imagine the pull of tidal water with a full moon that has caused the high spring tide straight ahead of you. The sun emerges over the sand dunes directly behind you. On an exposed sand bar you are part of a natural harmony, as you stand at the furthest magnetic pull of the tide.

" I have been coming to this beach ever since I was a baby. It is the place where I feel most relaxed, happiest, with a sense of space, with a beautiful view, come rain or shine; there's always something to look at and it just makes me feel very happy, for some reason. I love it. "

Padstow

 Parking available

 Toilets available

 Suffolk Coast Path

 Site of Special Scientific Interest

 Dogs allowed all year round

Scan me

> " I live about as far as you can get from the sea, so any opportunity I can get to come and inhale some sea air and listen to the gulls is absolutely magic for me. "

" We have the two large netters that are based in the port here, but in January to March we start to get beam trawlers that come around, because the Dover sole tend to migrate around this side of the coast and up to Liverpool Bay. It's quite exposed and we are lucky that we are up an estuary here, with the large north westerly swells that come in. "

The town of Padstow is a fine visitor attraction, as everywhere is walkable and grouped around the charming inner harbour. There are excellent shops, restaurants, hotels and pubs to hand, as well as a ferry across the river to beautiful Rock. However, if you look back up the River Camel towards Padstow from Stepper Point at the head of the estuary, you gain a fresh perspective and a reminder of Padstow's geographical context, providing rare shelter for boats on Cornwall's wild Atlantic coast. Although the town and inner harbour, with its tidal barrier, are quite a picture, it's worth remembering that fishing and Padstow's relationship with the sea are still highly valued.

Trevone

 Parking available

 Toilets available

 Suffolk Coast Path

 Site of Special Scientific Interest

 Dogs allowed (check locally)

 RNLI Lifeguard Cover (check locally)

 Beach cleaned regularly

Good water quality

Scan me

"From the point of
view of relaxing,
it's far better to be
on the beach than
anywhere else."

" When I walk onto this beach, it just makes my soul sing. Whenever I think of Trevone, I just think of happy, happy thoughts. Whatever the weather, we always get enjoyment out of this beach. "

Trevone is one in a string of exquisite beaches, with Mother Ivy's Bay, Harlyn Bay and Constantine Bay all close by. Visitors are protected by an RNLI crew who have a cabin at the top of the beach, where you'll also find parking. For me, an early morning visit to Trevone Bay is always a treat, especially on a low spring tide. On one such occasion, I remember the black rocks by the water's edge gleaming in the corner of my eye as I scanned across to Trevose lighthouse. When I looked around at these rocks by the beach I imagined them in their topographic context, as if I dived among them. Why not visit in the summer, to enjoy some leisure time under azure skies?

" Exhilarating, energising, salty sea air, waves crashing or gently lapping the beach, lying on the beach, digging your toes into the sand, or letting the sugar sand cascade through your fingers, standing on the smoothed rocks in bare feet hunting for creatures in the rock pools, spotting seals below the Round Hole, the sun dancing on your eyelashes as it sets into the sea, the feeling that Trevone has been there forever, and will be in the future, and I am so happy to have shared my life with such a wonderful place. "

Porthcothan

 Parking available

 Toilets available

 Suffolk Coast Path

 Dogs allowed all year round

 RNLI Lifeguard Cover (check locally)

 Beach cleaned regularly

 Good water quality

Scan me

"Well, it's everything really. It's an ecosystem, it's a place for recreation, it's treasured by the local people here. It instils a state of wonderment every time I come down – the different states of the beach, the tides, the sea. It's always changing. The sand dune is a unique piece of ecosystem on this part of the coast, with lizards, slow worms and other kinds of insects and butterflies."

" Offering immeasurable space, the beach stirs the
mind, body and soul unlike any other location. The
freedom it provides to run, play or just meander can
be found nowhere else. The sights, smells and sounds
are unique. They are held in the memories of any
child who has dipped their toes in the lapping waves,
skimmed a pebble across the surf, or encountered
the joy of melting, sand covered ice cream, dripping
down their chin. Proposals are written in the sand by
hopeful young men, dogs leap like racehorses across
the dunes. The day's worries are washed away like the
broken shells caught in the swell. The beach gives us
time to reflect, to be inspired, to enjoy. "

Arguably the best beachcombing location in Cornwall and home to
the late well-known filmmaker, beachcomber and fisherman Nick
Darke, Porthcothan is an unspoilt Atlantic beach. It attracts flotsam and
jetsam from as far away as the Amazon, riding in on the Gulf Stream. It
is a deep, rather than wide, beach. On a clear day, the weather-beaten
black rock stands starkly against a blue sky, an ocean scene interspersed
with the vivid white of rolling waves. On other occasions, perhaps deep in
winter, there is a subtle mix of grey, black and blue tones as the horizon
fuses into the sky and the elements collide. You can park across the road
from the back of the beach and there is a little shop by the dunes as you
approach the beach.

Crantock

 Parking available

 Toilets available

 Suffolk Coast Path

 Site of Special Scientific Interest

National Trust

 Dogs allowed all year round

 RNLI Lifeguard Cover (check locally)

 Beach cleaned regularly

Good water quality

Scan me

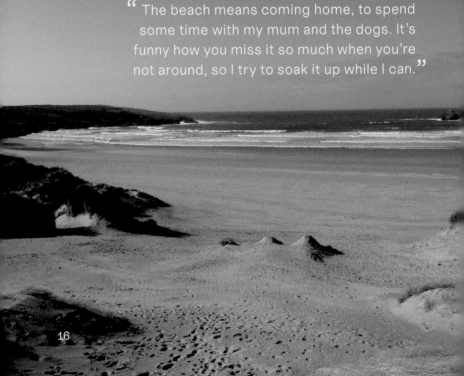

" The beach means coming home, to spend some time with my mum and the dogs. It's funny how you miss it so much when you're not around, so I try to soak it up while I can. "

"It means peace and quiet, solitude at times, a chance to get away from everyday problems, I suppose. We live in a city. It's a very busy lifestyle and now and again it's just great to be able to get away from it all, to walk the dog on the beach and it is a beautiful place."

Crantock beach is large and unspoilt. It is a National Trust beach with a large car park behind the tall dunes. If you look back to the beach from the end of either headland, the scene is theatrical, charismatic and wild. The beach itself maintains a breeze, even on the apparently stillest day and this gives any walk here an invigorating feel. The River Gannel runs to the sea across the beach, covering treacherous tides at its confluence with the Atlantic. On a wild day, to crouch in the lee of a rocky outcrop down by the water on East Pentire, as the wind howls above, is quite an experience. Only inches from the pounding Atlantic breakers, the early morning sun explodes out of the clouds to the left in golden shafts, lighting white horses on the storm-tossed waves. The sound is elemental, indescribable; unexpected walls of white water rise rhythmically between the torn rock at your feet. More than most, this is a beach that stays in your mind's eye long after you've left it.

"If ever I feel stressed, I just walk to the top of the sand dunes and look down onto glorious Crantock beach and the stresses melt away."

17

St Ives

 Parking available

 Toilets available

 Suffolk Coast Path

 Dogs allowed (check locally)

 Beach cleaned regularly

 Good water quality

Scan me

" The beach is where I do all my sailing from at the moment, primarily with a class of boat called a St Ives Jumbo, a traditional St Ives fishing boat from the late 1800s. They were designed specifically for this harbour. They dry out and they were smaller than most of the traditional working boats of the time. They were general purpose boats, designed to catch anything within easy reach of the harbour. "

" I've worked here all my life and it's a working harbour to me. It's a place where my grandfathers worked, fishing. Behind me is the lifeboat station and next year is the 75th anniversary of the lifeboat disaster in St Ives. My grandfather and his brother lost their life in that event, so there's an emotional tie to the harbour, there's a working tie to the harbour and also there's the enjoyment, the pleasure side of the harbour. "

St Ives is a popular, all year round getaway destination for city dwellers. It is compact and walkable, with four great beaches and plenty of hotels, restaurants, bars and cafes. The enclosed design of this harbour makes promenading a pleasure at any time of day or in the evening. An early morning visit, to see the sun rise beyond Smeaton's Pier over Hayle Towans across the bay, is a real treat. St Ives retains its fishing heritage. I remember one occasion when glistening mackerel were being landed in modest numbers on Smeaton's Pier as the tide started to fall back. The fine sand of the beach shone under the gentle lapping of the harbour waves, a timeless scene shared with the fishermen before the town woke up. There is a rich maritime history here and a fine RNLI presence to save lives at sea.

19

Porthmeor

 Parking available

 Toilets available

 Suffolk Coast Path

 Site of Special Scientific Interest

 Dogs allowed (check locally)

 RNLI Lifeguard Cover (check locally)

 Beach cleaned regularly

 Good water quality

Scan me

> " I get drawn back to the beach because of its mysteries and its possibilities, so it has something almost magical about it. I just look beyond the sea and maybe think, maybe dream about what there might be. "

"It's just a place where you can always be at one. You don't know where the gap ends between the land and the sea. It's just really peaceful. It eats into your soul. You don't know where it comes from. It's just an elemental dynamic. There is nothing more powerful than the sea."

Backed by the popular Tate St Ives gallery, this is the most well-known St Ives beach, with the best surf. I recommend the view from the headland below St Nicholas' Chapel, showcasing the depth of the beach's bay and its place on the edge of the town. There's a great walk round to the west from here. There is a rural, almost primeval feel as you make your way along towards Zennor and Morvah, part of wild Penwith. I remember one winter visit. The morning sun was low. It lit the waves out at sea but hadn't yet reached the sand. The contrast was striking, highlighted by the white foam of the surf against the dark, golden sand. The white sea spray against the black rocks created a dramatic contrast. On another occasion it was a bright end to the day, with the sun starting to sink in the west over the beach. There were still plenty of people on the beach, but the beachside cafe was full and well-heeled partygoers promenaded, anticipating the pleasures of St Ives in the evening.

Sennen Cove

 Parking available

 Toilets available

 Suffolk Coast Path

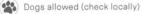 Dogs allowed (check locally)

 RNLI Lifeguard Cover (check locally)

 Good water quality

Scan me

Sitting at the far western end of the county, Sennen Cove features wild nature and waves as well as art and craft shops, plus a harbour with a lifeboat. Whitesand Bay, by Sennen Cove, is a fine sight on a low tide, since it is one of Cornwall's flattest and most scenic beaches. The beach arcs round to the headland and the raking backdrop is natural, primeval and unspoilt. The sea breeze from the Atlantic is bracing and pure here at the tip of these beautiful islands. There is a sense of the sea's power playing across the western tip of Cornwall, heady and stimulating, especially when viewed from the shelter of the harbour.

" For many years I had to commute to London every week to work. Weekends spent on Sennen beach, with the smell of ozone in the air, the soft sand underfoot, swimming in the sea on a warm day or watching the surfers who were there in all winds and weathers – this was what revived me enough to get back in the car on a Sunday night. Now I'm back here full time, I realise how lucky I am to live in such a beautiful place. **"**

Porthcurno

 Parking available

 Dogs allowed (check locally)

 Toilets available

 RNLI Lifeguard Cover (check locally)

 Suffolk Coast Path

 Beach cleaned regularly

 Site of Special Scientific Interest

Good water quality

Scan me

" The beach means everything to me. We are always drawn to the beach. We come down here as much as we can. All of the time that you are working hard, you are part of the big machine. As soon as you come back to the beach, you realise there is a lot more to life than just work. "

> " It looks really lovely. The tamarisk is coming out now and the honeysuckle is just starting to come into leaf. There are primroses all around the edge here, a few gulls flying, very peaceful. "

This is one of the most beautiful, pristine beaches in Cornwall. It sits below the Minack Theatre, which is carved into the cliffs above. Standing at the head of the beach is the tiny cable house designed to help to send telegrams to America,. There are very impressive square blocks of granite in the western cliffs, almost pink in a certain light. In high summer I remember a calm sea shining silver, the breakers almost translucent as they arched and fell on the golden sand. Visitors milled about. You could sense the pressure lifting from their shoulders as they walked the beach or sat gazing out to sea. They couldn't have found a finer spot. This is a magical beach in any weather and season, nestled on a finger of land by the wide Atlantic Ocean.

> " The colours of the sea at Porthcurno never cease to amaze me – the white sand is made up almost entirely of tiny, 30,000 year old seashells which extend well below the water line, giving the sea a bright turquoise colour – you could be mistaken for thinking you are in the Caribbean. Having travelled the world during my time with British Airways, Porthcurno beach is hard to beat! "

Penzance Mount's Bay

 Parking available

 Toilets available

 Suffolk Coast Path

 Dogs allowed all year round

 RNLI Lifeguard Cover (check locally)

 Beach cleaned regularly

 Good water quality

Scan me

"This is called Battery Rocks because there did used to be a battery here during Napoleonic times, a battery of cannons. St. Michael's Mount, Cudden Point and The Lizard in the far distance — I can pick out all sorts of things here. Yes, it's a good view. You can see Goonhilly Satellite Tracking station in the distance, to the right of it is Loe Bar."

" The beach a place where I'm reminded that all my problems are so small that they're not worth worrying about – it puts everything into perspective. The waves will come and go, the tideline will move and no amount of worrying will stop them. Flinging off my shoes and losing a couple of hours throwing a ball for the dog or paddling about in rock pools is like therapy, I always leave the beach happy and content with the world. "

Located towards the western end of Mount's Bay, Penzance's seafront is an ideal spot to grasp the scale of the bay, which runs from beyond Marazion in the east to Newlyn and Mousehole in the west. This is the departure point for the Scillonian ferry to the Scilly Isles. The promenade leads you round to the Lido and Battery Rocks, a popular spot for sea swimmers. On a calm day, the sea glistens silver, framing St Michael's Mount in the light. The sound of the pebbles rolling back on the ebb of the tide is rejuvenating and the light here is unique, as captured in the paintings of the Newlyn School of Art's Stanhope Forbes and Henry Scott Tuke. At Penzance you have choices, to watch the world go by, walk the promenade or exercise in the sea.

Perranuthnoe

 Parking available

 Toilets available

 Suffolk Coast Path

 Dogs allowed all year round

 Good water quality

Scan me

> " We've been coming to this beach since 1969. It brings back lots and lots of memories, memories of being with my husband's grandfather, memories of bringing his dog here, memories of bringing our children here, who are now thirty downwards. "

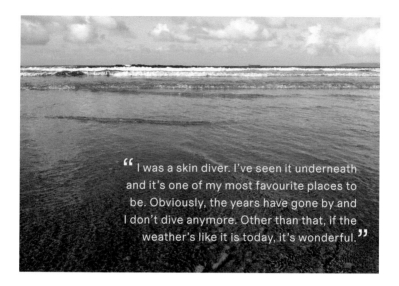

" I was a skin diver. I've seen it underneath and it's one of my most favourite places to be. Obviously, the years have gone by and I don't dive anymore. Other than that, if the weather's like it is today, it's wonderful. "

Perranuthnoe is not one of Cornwall's most heralded beaches, yet its location between Mount's Bay and Praa Sands is spectacular. There is usually plenty of space to walk in peace as well as fine views out to sea in both directions. The cliff walk round to Mount's Bay is memorable. The Cabin cafe is handy for food and drink, located just behind the beach. On one springtime visit, the soft cliffs at the back of the beach had been carved out by the winter storms, leaving them twenty feet back from their position when I was last here. Seaweed was strewn on the beach, an ever-changing sensory experience, full of drama and energy. On another occasion, during a bright summer's morning, the ebb tide left a sheen on the sand. Out at sea, inshore fishing boats collected their pots and looked for mackerel. This is indeed a magical place.

Praa Sands

 Parking available

 Dogs allowed (check locally)

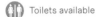 Toilets available

 RNLI Lifeguard Cover (check locally)

 Suffolk Coast Path

 Beach cleaned regularly

 Site of Special Scientific Interest

Good water quality

 Scan me

"For us, the beach means well-being; a time to take a breath, look to the horizon, dip a toe (or more) into the revitalising sea and spend time connecting back to nature and to ourselves."

" Today I went down to the beach and it's like looking out towards the end of the world. It brings to me just how insignificant we really are and how magnificent everything is. When we're feeling pretty self-important, it brings us back to where we should be. **"**

Along with Kennack Sands, this is the preferred choice for surfers when North Coast conditions are unfavourable, since it also catches the long North Atlantic swell. Access to the beach is excellent, with parking, a short links golf course, a beach cafe, restaurants and shops all available. There are rock pools at the end of the beach, with fine views across to St Michael's Mount and Mount's Bay, as well as good access to the South West Coast Path. The beach is sandy and flat, ideal for a dog walk at any time of the day.

Poldhu Cove

 Parking available

 Toilets available

 Suffolk Coast Path

 Site of Special Scientific Interest

 Dogs allowed (check locally)

 RNLI Lifeguard Cover (check locally)

 Beach cleaned regularly

Good water quality

 Scan me

" I live on the beach, I've worked on the beach for thirty-five years, I'm probably addicted to the beach. If I've had two days away from the beach, I have to get back. So it means addiction. I'm going to try and fight it, but not too hard. "

This is a magnificent, untamed beach, which faces the Atlantic on the western side of the Lizard Peninsula. Perhaps its isolated location, near to RNAS Culdrose and through the village of Gunwalloe, plus the fact that you don't just pass by it, rather you must want to go to it, makes it such an enviable destination. On arrival, Poldhu Cove has the feel of a North Coast beach. At low tide the beach is surprisingly expansive and its flat demeanour leaves intricate swirls in the sand, such is the speed of the tidal race. The rocks by the side of the beach have been blasted and sculpted by the Atlantic, a wonder to enjoy at low tide. This is a great place to reflect in a pristine environment, surrounded by nature. There is a charm and a welcoming karma. In truth, it's hard to pull yourself away from Poldhu Cove.

" As I got older, I remember lazy summer days there with friends and tipsy evenings with the same friends. I can see why visitors are compelled to come back, year after year. Some even love it so much they move to this corner of the world. To me, Poldhu means memories, good times, friends and family. Poldhu means home. "

Kynance Cove

 Parking available

 Toilets available

 Suffolk Coast Path

 The Lizard National Nature Reserve

 Site of Special Scientific Interest

 National Trust

 Dogs allowed
(check locally)

 Scan me

Consistently among the most viewed beach pages at manonabeach. com, Kynance Cove is for many people the quintessential Cornish cove and beach. Its combination of characterful islands, serpentine-laced caves, a blow hole and pristine beaches make this a special place. I have encountered visitors experiencing a natural "high" here and it's intoxicating. The best time to visit is on an ebb tide towards low tide when it is safe to scramble around the nooks and crannies. If you are ever fortunate, as I was once, to be the first person on this beach in the morning, you may witness the tide turn inward and your footsteps will be washed away, the beach assuming another guise as it has done throughout time. When looking out to the Atlantic from such an exposed place, it seems to me a tempting horizon, beyond which lays new adventures and acquaintances, new suggestions and implications, new challenges and opportunities.

"For me, it means peace and tranquillity. Every time the waves come in and go out, it feels as though any of my worries are just washed away. The clean sand is like the purity and the waves are the cleansing nature."

Lizard Point

 Parking available

 Toilets available

 Suffolk Coast Path

 Site of Special Scientific Interest

 National Trust

 Dogs allowed all year round

 Scan me

> " It does mean a lot. It brings back loads of memories and we love it. The light is special and it's good for painting down here."

Lizard Point, the most southerly land in Britain, has a small beach next to the old lifeboat house. There are many good reasons to visit, from the serpentine shops and Polpeor cafe to the local wildlife, which includes seals, choughs and adders. The Lizard lighthouse is spectacular, and you have easy access to Bass Point, the Lloyds telegraph building and the Marconi wireless hut, as well as the South West Coast Path. There is a youth hostel too, and it is an easy walk to Lizard village. I remember an early morning visit. Heavy dew on the cliff-side grass provided the counterpoint to the clear air, full of the scent of wild garlic. Sea pink and primroses abounded and I photographed both a transient snail and an adder on the coast path. On another visit the tide crashed against the rocks as gulls, crows, jays and a lone chough circled above the fields next to the cliffs. This part of the county has different geology to the rest of Cornwall, hence the serpentine you find in caves nearby at Kynance Cove.

" The Lizard is a unique spot. Some of the rock formations in this area are among the oldest on earth. A vein of serpentine runs across the area, a rock worked by local people. "

Cadgwith

 Parking available

 Toilets available

 Suffolk Coast Path

 Dogs allowed all year round

 Site of Special Scientific Interest

Scan me

> " Well, it's home for me. I've been here all my life. I'm drawn down to the beach. "

It's not by accident that access to villages like Cadgwith, Mousehole, Mevagissey and Fowey is tricky by road. They are all designed to be approached from the sea and each house points out to the sea, the traditional source of income. The little inshore fleet at Cadgwith is still viable, but it is now part of a smaller Cornish and UK fishing fleet. Nowadays visitors enjoy looking back towards these harbours from the headlands, usually from part of the excellent South West Coast Path. The fishing boats, drawn up on the hard standing, seem to fascinate people, perhaps tapping deeply into a lost association we all have with the coast, looking back through our history as island people. I remember one visit, standing on the end of the Todden in Cadgwith. Time seemed to stand still as the morning sun broke through the sky onto the two small beaches here. A high tide was starting to fall away and a blanket of white ebbed and flowed over the black rock of the headlands. All the boats were pulled right up the hard standing, with one even parked on the road next to a thatched cottage. Time had parked me between two ages.

> " The beach is the heart of the local community, of both Cadgwith and Ruan Minor, where I live. It's a place of enjoyment, a place of activity where all the fishing boats are. "

Gyllyngvase

 Parking available

 Toilets available

 Suffolk Coast Path

 Dogs allowed (check locally)

 RNLI Lifeguard Cover (check locally)

 Beach cleaned regularly

 Good water quality

Scan me

"Sometimes I wonder 'Why do I swim?' and each day it is a different answer. Sometimes I feel it is only water and other times I think it is everything, sea, sky and everything beneath me."

It's always a pleasure to visit this high octane Falmouth beach, particularly on a bright weekend morning, when it's a hive of activity. As a town beach it holds a natural attraction for locals, with volleyball nets, a popular cafe and a safe swimming environment. There is plenty of space for everyone, in and out of the water. With pleasant gardens by the beach, there are fine views to enjoy over Falmouth Bay, all the way round from Pendennis Castle to the Helford Estuary. My first impression of Gyllyngvase is always that it is a hive of activity for locals and visitors alike. The strongest draw are the elements in Falmouth Bay. On one chilly early spring morning, icy winds and a morning chill set the tone. An ebb tide clawed at the sand leaving thirty feet of sea trace before returning it to visible beach. Above the sea, an apocalyptic sky, with clouds full of snow, threatened to add its contents to the elemental mix.

" Freedom and a safe place for my children to run around. There is lots of sea glass, which we are collecting to make pictures when we get home. It is weathered pieces of glass that have been in the sea and they are quite smooth. We make sea designs from it, all washed up on the beach for free. **"**

Restronguet Passage

 Dogs allowed all year round

Scan me

" The beach is my childhood. Whether turning stones to see what
I could find, or catching eels and crabs from the pontoon. Also,
the old oyster fishermen featured heavily in my early years.
Restronguet Creek is home. I just love it. "

Restronguet Passage includes areas of crag and beach, running from Weir beach up towards the Pandora Inn and the Carnon River beyond. There's always plenty to see here, whether you're looking across to Turnaware Beach and the Roseland Peninsula or towards Restronguet Point itself. The winding lane and path are tree-covered and feel secretive, offering glimpses of outstanding natural beauty across the water as you ramble along, plus on one occasion for me, a rainbow. I also remember feeling nostalgic standing by the famous Pandora Inn on a dull October morning. I looked across through the swinging moorings to the houses on Restronguet Point at the top of Carrick Roads. Despite the occasional glimpse of a sail-driven oyster dredger, this is now a leisure waterway, very different from the industrial scenes of drag mining across the Carnon River hundreds of years ago.

" Oh, many happy memories from over the years, of coming down here early in the morning with my young son and seeing it in each mood, each season of the year. If you get there early in the morning, it may seem anti-social, but I like it that way. You can take everything in without clutter and sound, just the natural noises around you. "

St Mawes

 Parking available

 Toilets available

 Suffolk Coast Path

 Dogs allowed all year round

 Scan me

" It's the most beautiful, peaceful place. I come back two or three times a year and whatever the weather I am down here, collecting shells, swimming. It's just beautiful. It speaks for itself, the light on the water, especially early in the morning, it's absolutely stunning. This is my favourite time, when no-one else is here. "

14

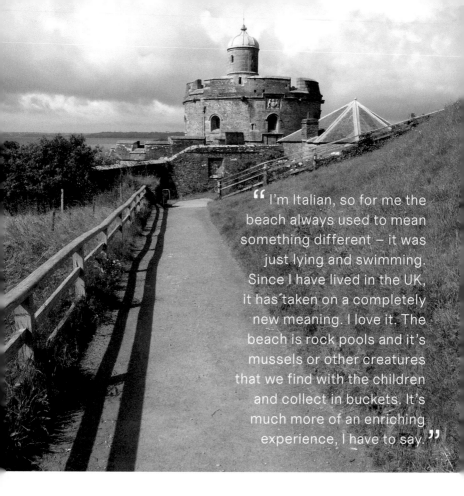

" I'm Italian, so for me the beach always used to mean something different – it was just lying and swimming. Since I have lived in the UK, it has taken on a completely new meaning. I love it. The beach is rock pools and it's mussels or other creatures that we find with the children and collect in buckets. It's much more of an enriching experience, I have to say. "

This upmarket village sits near to the southern tip of the Roseland Peninsula. St Mawes has excellent shops, hotels, art galleries, restaurants and pubs, as well as a post office and a delicatessen. The daytime views across Carrick Roads or up the Percuil River are second to none, and the town feels very welcoming. Heritage sailing is a feature of playtime here and there is a thriving sailing club, which supports local classes such as the St Mawes One Design, Ajax and Sunbeam. Linked with Falmouth, there is heritage sailing aboard the working boats, some dating back to the nineteenth century.

Portscatho

 Parking available

 Toilets available

 South West Coast Path

 Dogs allowed all year round

Scan me

" It's a wonderful place to walk my dog, but more than that it's the sea and how it draws you out of yourself and gives you a great sense of the vastness of the world and makes me feel very peaceful. "

46

This east-facing village on the Roseland Peninsula is connected to the village of Gerrans and each village has a pub. Once a thriving fishing village, Portscatho now features art galleries, a cafe, a gift shop and an excellent general store, incorporating a post office. With its picturesque setting, it's easy to see why Portscatho has become so popular with visitors and retirees alike. There is still a modest commercial fishing presence to supply the tourist industry and the nearby upmarket hotels at Rosevine. With a choice of beaches, there is plenty on offer for families, with rock pools and building sandcastles.

" I'm the harbourmaster here so it's part of my livelihood.
As a family, we fish and farm in the area. We fish from
Portscatho in the boats over here in the harbour and we
farm just along the coast, so 'quite a lot' is the answer
to that." ("What does the beach mean to you...?") **"**

47

Pendower

 Parking available

 Toilets available

 Suffolk Coast Path

 Site of Special Scientific Interest

 Dogs allowed all year round

 Beach cleaned regularly

 Good water quality

Scan me

> " This is somewhere I can come and unwind with my family during the summer months and during the winter months. It's just so beautiful. We thoroughly enjoy it, every minute that we are down here. "

" It's the reason we moved to Cornwall. We used to come down here when the children were little and my parents had moved down, about thirty-five years ago. This is what we had dreamed about. We moved down and we absolutely love it. "

There's an uncanny benevolence at this beach. Facing south as it looks out over Gerrans Bay, it is half of a long strand that includes the adjacent Carne beach. Its varied topology is also interesting, with trees, dunes, a river, eroded rocks, sand and the ocean all in proximity. Perhaps it's this variety of sensory stimuli that evokes such a feeling of contentment here. A dawn visit to Pendower beach two days before the summer solstice showcased moody, atmospheric elements. A lone dog walker accompanied me for this 5.15 am sojourn. Since the sky tends to the apocalyptic at the mildest of times at Pendower, there was a wild, dark cloak of sky and sun over the beach on this occasion, yet the sea was placid and calm. The tide was half in, with lime green rocks still visible on the shoreline. A river runs down to join the sea across this exquisite beach.

Carne

 Parking available

 Toilets available

 Suffolk Coast Path

 Site of Special Scientific Interest

 Dogs allowed all year round

 Beach cleaned regularly

 Good water quality

Scan me

" If it wasn't here, I'd go crazy. I can walk my dogs in the winter, so it means a lot to me. I'm a beachy person, not in the sense of sunbathing, but just walking along the beach. It's just beautiful. "

" As a person who lives in the middle of this wonderful country of ours, I enjoy going to the beaches. It makes me feel happy and healthy and I'm going to go back home this morning to Shropshire, having enjoyed my few days on the beach. "

Sharing the strand with Pendower beach to the west, try to catch Carne beach early in the morning to see the dawn light emerging behind the Nare Head in the east and falling across a pristine beach. As well as having rock pools to explore at the eastern end of Carne, both beaches are popular for sea swimming and windsurfing too due to their flat, expansive nature and the enveloping bay. Dramatic winter storms often impact the soft cliffs behind the beach. I like to visit when the seasonal wheel turns from summer to autumn. At that time a frenetic mixture of the two seasons is commonplace, warm yet with a precocious breeze that gusts through the scudding black and grey clouds. The white tops of the waves are set in relief by the grey tones around them. It is a time of temperate flux, foreshadowing the seasonal change.

51

Porthluney

 Parking available

 Toilets available

 Suffolk Coast Path

 Site of Special Scientific Interest

 Dogs allowed all year round

 Beach cleaned regularly

 Good water quality

Scan me

> " It's just openness, isn't it? The open air and the sun and the sea. Peacefulness. The waves can be calm, or they can be ferocious, depending on what day it is, really. They are either deadly or they're calm, a bit like a lot of people. "

" You can use the beach annually, which is great. It's not just the beach, it's also the sea, all part of the coastline. You can find things that have been washed in from miles away, Nova Scotia, the Caribbean, so it's exciting, beachcombing. I also enjoy the birdlife and the mammals, the seals. "

The steep sides to the beach belie the deceptively wide expanse of sand at Porthluney, which is a safe bathing beach with clean water all year round. Beside the beach is Caerhays Castle where the first *Williamsii camellia* were propagated from *Camellia japonica* by Carolyn Williams. The coastline here between the Dodman Point and the Nare Head is some of the least spoilt on the south coast of Cornwall. On one occasion I remember the tide rising deceptively quickly over the flat beach, scattering the foraging birds on the sand at the water's edge into clouds. Tall pines cover traces of the headlands' rough grazing partitions, where orchards once decorated the cliff sides. In winter water thunders onto the beach from a swollen river, dissipating to wander languidly across the wide beach, down to the endless sea.

Portmellon

 Parking available

 Toilets available

 Suffolk Coast Path

 Dogs allowed all year round

 Good water quality

 Scan me

> It means a letting out of pressure when I walk the dog in the day and the evening. When you come on a summer's day with the sand, it's a frivolous place. You relax completely. But on a wild day it can be a challenge, so it's a contradiction.

54

" I just adore it. One day it's like a mill pool and the water is as clear as tap water. Another day, the easterly wind comes and it crashes on the wall and the spray clears the houses. It's just a magical place. This is where my heart is and stays all the year, although I only have it for two weeks. "

The easterly aspect at Portmellon makes it a fine beach to visit in the morning. It sits on an inlet between Mevagissey to the north and Gorran Haven to the south, just beyond Chapel Point. Colona House guards the northern edge of the inlet, with the idyllic Chapel Point at the other end. Most people here live on a hill behind the beach and road, which is just as well because an easterly storm regularly crosses the road and bombards the beach-side houses, strewing seaweed over the road and any passing cars. It's hard to overstate the beauty of a sunrise at Portmellon. The scene is framed by the two headlands as you look out over the bay. The overall impression is both expansive and intimate, an exquisite contradiction.

Readymoney Cove

 Toilets available

 Dogs allowed (check locally)

 Scan me

" The beach is a place of tranquillity, calm, spiritual uplifting. No matter how you feel, you can always come to the beach and you feel something. I see the sun, the waves, it's absolutely beautiful, untouched, nature at its best. "

56

" It can change my mood, because the sea and the beach is always different. The sea changes everything. It has a calming effect. You can do so much on the beach. I love watching the children playing on the beach. It's something for everybody, old people, children, it's magic. "

Readymoney Cove is the beach for Fowey, itself one of Cornwall's upmarket visitor attractions. At the estuary of the River Fowey, the Tudor St Catherine's Castle commands the entrance to Fowey, located just above this beach. There is a tranquil, detached romanticism about Readymoney Cove, despite its immediate proximity to a busy town. A bungalow inhabited by Daphne du Maurier sits just behind the beach. It is popular for swimming and a pontoon is rigged up in the summer just below the castle. A summer highlight is Fowey Week in August, when you can enjoy the spectacle of the Falmouth working boats racing in the estuary, showing their colourful topsails. A more genteel alternative is the excellent Fowey Festival of Arts and Literature, usually held in May.

Great Lantic

 Parking available

 Suffolk Coast Path

 Dogs allowed all year round

 Site of Special Scientific Interest

Scan me

"It's one of the most exhilarating and beautiful beaches in the whole of Southern Cornwall."

Sitting between Polruan to the west and Polperro to the east, this magical beach is difficult to access down a steep path but it is well worth the effort. The nature here is pristine and on a fine day Lantic Bay is serene and tranquil, with clear turquoises and blues in the sea and sky. In summer the upper beach vegetation is in bloom. On the high ridge above the beach you will find ardent walkers enjoying the South West Coast Path, the odd one dropping down for a well-earned rest on this beautiful beach. This side of the Fowey River estuary has wonderful sea views looking out from the high cliffs, as well as beautiful, wild beaches. It's totally wild, unspoilt and timeless, without commercial intrusion. The geology is fascinating, with creased, folded and eroded rock formations standing proud against the relentless assault of the ocean.

"It's looking at the sea for me and looking a long distance. We have a yearning for the sea. It's good looking out at it and seeing the horizon. You don't often see that in a city. "

Seaton

 Parking available

 Toilets available

 Suffolk Coast Path

 Dogs allowed (check locally)

 Beach cleaned regularly

Good water quality

Scan me

" For me, the beach is a place to escape everyday life and experience the power and beauty of nature. Whether I'm in the mood for quiet contemplation, a vigorous walk or just some relaxing fun, it stimulates the senses and reminds me what's important. "

" I love the beach. I come most days to run and particularly to do yoga right on the seashore, where the waves are lapping. It's so great, because all the elements are here on the beach and I really connect with the grounding of the earth, the potentiality and the expansion of the water, the warmth of the sun and the fire. "

Seaton and its beach lie tucked away in the quiet southeast corner of Cornwall at the entrance to the Seaton Valley Country Park, where otters and butterflies can be seen. This is a part of the county that is well worth visiting for this fact alone, but there is also great scenic beauty here. The South West Coast Path passes the beach, leading west towards Looe or east towards Downderry and beyond. A river runs across the shingle to the sea, carving the beach in half and there is a smart beach cafe at the head of the beach. The beach is popular with dog walkers and young families, but oddly it is one of a few south coast Cornwall beaches where you can surf.

Whitsand Bay

 Parking available

 Dogs allowed all year round

 Toilets available

 RNLI Lifeguard Cover (check locally)

 Suffolk Coast Path

 Good water quality

 Site of Special Scientific Interest

Scan me

" I think the beach means to me peace and quiet, tranquillity and calm. "

" The beach means all the world to me. I've been coming here since I was a baby with my parents. They met here. I came here as a teenager; I came here with my children and now I bring my grandchildren here. "

Whitsand Bay runs north from Rame Head in Cornwall's southeast corner. It's a long beach that faces west and comprises several smaller beaches, each with its own character and its own patrons. Above the beach is the nineteenth-century Tregantle Fort, designed at Lord Palmerston's initiative to protect the channel ports from French attack. There are beach houses that cling to the steep cliffs above. Due to Plymouth's proximity this is also a much-visited beauty spot, despite its steep access. Once, on a falling tide, I visited the most popular section of beach in front of the Eddystone cafe. This part of the beach is staggeringly beautiful and wild. On that occasion, the low tide made the pristine beach accessible, with a chance to see a modern warship cruising close by the shore.

Devon and Dorset

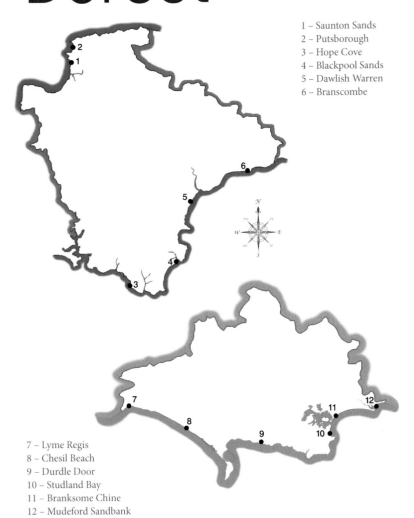

1 – Saunton Sands
2 – Putsborough
3 – Hope Cove
4 – Blackpool Sands
5 – Dawlish Warren
6 – Branscombe

7 – Lyme Regis
8 – Chesil Beach
9 – Durdle Door
10 – Studland Bay
11 – Branksome Chine
12 – Mudeford Sandbank

Saunton Sands

 Parking available

 Dogs allowed (check locally)

 Toilets available

 Beach cleaned regularly

 South West Coast Path

 Good water quality

 Site of Special Scientific Interest

Scan me

" At every opportunity I head to the beach! We have a motorhome called Calamity and a dog called Charliechops and have found some superb beaches. We went to Braunton in North Devon in June and discovered Saunton Sands beach, which is dog friendly and a fantastic space to walk for miles, grabbing a coffee and a bite at the beach cafe at the end of it! Perfect. "

Saunton Sands is an expansive west-facing beach, located just below Croyde and almost three miles in length. It's in a stunning location with Braunton Burrows, a UNESCO Biosphere Reserve, located immediately behind the beach. There are excellent coastal walks and attractive villages nearby. The beach has a tidal range of 8.5 metres and is well known for its languid, long waves. Although it is a safe and popular swimming beach, care is needed when swimming due to a lack of RNLI cover. This beach is unspoilt and dogs are welcome at all times of the year. On a fine day the sea is azure when viewed from the road above the cliff next to the beach and the sand is soft and golden. Nearby Braunton has plenty of shops and facilities.

" The beach is pretty much half my life. I walk the dog
here every morning with my wife and I think that's
a very important time for us. My kids are in the Surf
Life Saving Club here. I'm in the Surf Life Saving
Club here. The beach is a big part of my life. "

" Saunton Sands and Woolacombe are two of my favourite
places in the world. The beach gives me a real sense of
being a part of a much bigger world. I love being on the
beach – whatever time of the day and whatever season of
the year. The beaches in Devon offer an incredible sense
of calm which allow you to unwind and lose yourself.
There is nowhere I'd rather be than on the beach. Hoorah
for Devon beaches, what a lucky lot we are.... "

67

Putsborough

 Parking available

 Toilets available

South West Coast Path

 Site of Special Scientific Interest

 Dogs allowed (check locally)

 Beach cleaned regularly

 Good water quality

Scan me

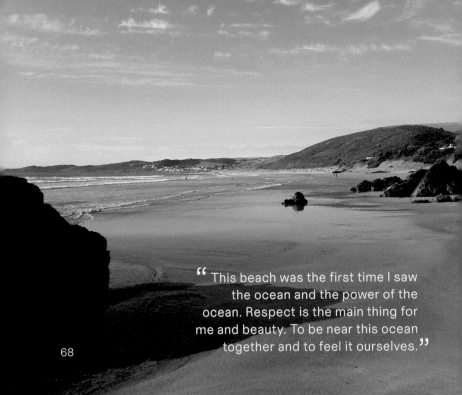

" This beach was the first time I saw the ocean and the power of the ocean. Respect is the main thing for me and beauty. To be near this ocean together and to feel it ourselves. "

" For me, the beach and particularly this beach means getting close to the forces of nature, looking at how we're so insignificant, the formation of the rocks and how they were shaped by the water, the colours, the noise; it's just beautiful. I draw power from this. It revitalises me. "

To the north of Putsborough beach are Woolacombe and Morte Point with Baggy Point to the south. This is one of the finest stretches of sand in the southwest, three miles long in total. There is a tranquil ambience here. It is unspoilt and a place of great beauty. Thanks to the protection of Baggy Point, the beach is sheltered from the prevailing south westerly winds. It attracts water sports enthusiasts, particularly surfers and kayakers. There are rock pools for children to explore. The sea is clean and safe for bathing and there is fine walking hereabouts on the South West Coast Path. Dogs are welcome to the right of the steps down to the beach between October and April.

Hope Cove

 Parking available

 Toilets available

South West Coast Path

 Site of Special Scientific Interest

 National Trust

 Dogs allowed (check locally)

 Beach cleaned regularly

Good water quality

Scan me

" It means memories, peaceful, relaxing, unchanging. "

"I like the colours on this beach. I like the sound of the birds and the wildlife. Sometimes it gets really stormy and the waves break over there. It is an atmospheric place, not exactly haunted, but full of feelings of old fisherfolk. You can feel it from the rocks, I think. I like colours and I like feelings."

Hope Cove, comprising Inner and Outer Hope, nestles beneath dramatic cliffs in front of the sharp eroded rocks which lie just offshore. An exceptionally scenic part of the South West Coast Path passes above the beach and there are plenty of facilities immediately behind the cove. The coast here is part of a Site of Special Scientific Interest, and both peregrine falcons and kestrels can be found just inland among the greenery. Hope Cove is cared for the National Trust. There is also a rich maritime history featuring the wreck of a Spanish galleon in Tudor times, as well as the loss of 708 souls on HMS Ramillie in 1760. A notable smuggling area, fishermen collected barrels of brandy from the seabed in far flung days. Hope Cove is an affluent part of the South Hams where restaurants and the hotel do a brisk trade. There are views across to Burgh Island and Bigbury-on-Sea from Outer Hope, the cliffs adding a fine perspective to both beaches.

Blackpool Sands

 Parking available

 Toilets available

 South West Coast Path

 Dogs allowed (check locally)

 RNLI Lifeguard Cover (check locally)

 Beach cleaned regularly

 Good water quality

Scan me

"I think it means memories, fun, sandcastles, swimming, early mornings like today, general family fun."

This crescent-shaped, golden sandy beach is the most easterly of the South Devon beaches. A wonderful backdrop of cliffs, trees and greenery attracts families with children, many of whom return through the generations with their own young ones. This is a Blue Flag Award-winning beach with unusually clear water, a bather's paradise. Blackpool Sands is privately and fastidiously managed with showers, a sandpit for children and many other facilities for visitors. Kayaks, paddleboards and wetsuits are all for hire here. The beach sits in front of the South West Coast Path. Why not try the excellent circular walk from the beach to Stoke Fleming via a thirteenth-century church and the Green Dragon pub which has commanding views out to sea?

"If I could put it into one word, it would be thankful. We have this wonderful place on our doorstep to run and exercise on. Also, I'm thankful because, blimey, it's just nice to be fit enough to do this. I also feel grateful that we have such wonderful people here. It's like just friends, we're all supporting each other."

Dawlish Warren

 Parking available

 Dogs allowed (check locally)

 Toilets available

 RNLI Lifeguard Cover (check locally)

South West Coast Path

Beach cleaned regularly

 Dawlish Warren National Nature Reserve

 Good water quality

 Scan me

"The beach changes every time I come down. I love walking by the beach and walking on the sand every day. It's a lot quieter than Dawlish itself. At the beach, young children don't need any other entertainment. With a bucket and spade, they are happy for hours."

❝ The beach was always a great place to go to spend long summer days swimming and snorkelling over the rocks. I thoroughly enjoyed that. We used to come to Dawlish Warren on the ferry from Exmouth to Starcross with a bike and cycle on to the Warren. Dawlish Warren has a bird hide, with migrating birds that come through in the autumn and in the spring. It's a lovely place to be. ❞

Sitting opposite Exmouth across the Exe Estuary, Dawlish Warren beach is almost a mile long. Behind the attractive, sandy beach is Dawlish Warren National Nature Reserve, a wildlife sanctuary by the sea that can boast of over six hundred species of flowering plants in its grassland. Rangers supervise pond-dipping and give tours of the reserve. Nearby Dawlish offers further coastal views and excellent shopping for visitors. There are fine views across a silver sea towards Exmouth in the east, while ancient desert sand cliffs frame the main railway line towards Teignmouth to the west. Some groynes on the beach have been removed under the Beach Management Scheme, as the movement of sand and shore hereabouts is constantly managed.

Branscombe

 Parking available

 Toilets available

 South West Coast Path

 Dogs allowed (check locally)

 RNLI Lifeguard Cover (check locally)

 Beach cleaned regularly

 Good water quality

 Scan me

" The beach is the place where I bring my dog every morning. It's also the place where I feel very good. I think human beings are like little electrical, chemical machines and sometimes you get too much electricity inside you and you need to be earthed. **"**

Branscombe beach sits in front of the picturesque village of Branscombe. There is parking by the beach but I prefer to approach on foot, either along the valley by the peaceful path or by climbing to the ridge and approaching from above. The high road leads you through gorgeous deciduous woodland, opening up to reveal the shingle beach and the ocean below. The pebble strand stretches along to Beer Head in the east; the South West Coast Path above the beach is a spectacular alternative, itself offering far-reaching views. Boats can be hired for pleasure and fishing trips run from the beach. Like several beaches in Suffolk, this part of East Devon is a great place to collect hag stones, where smaller stones have worn a hole in a larger stone through the sea's motions over time. Local folklore says you should keep one with you to ward off evil spirits.

" I like walking along the beach. I now know what a hag stone is and I have found two. I think I can say I'm hooked, because now there is a purpose to walking along the beach, to look for these stones. Lovely to meet you. **"**

Lyme Regis

 Parking available

 Toilets available

 South West Coast Path

 Site of Special Scientific Interest

 Dogs allowed (check locally)

 RNLI Lifeguard Cover (check locally)

 Beach cleaned regularly

Good water quality

Scan me

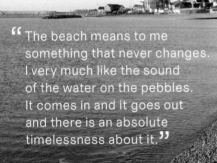

"The beach means to me
something that never changes.
I very much like the sound
of the water on the pebbles.
It comes in and it goes out
and there is an absolute
timelessness about it."

"I think the beach and the seaside mean freedom and escape."

Lyme Regis has fine scenery, making it an appealing resort to visit at any time of the year. Its historic Cobb and the harbour are revered features and the town sits among moody blue cliffs that yield fossilised evidence of life on earth millions of years ago. The town was mentioned in The Domesday Book and is home to several historical landmarks and educational attractions. As well as providing the inspiration for Tolkien's *The Hobbit*, the harbour has featured in film adaptations of John Fowles' *French Lieutenant's Woman* and Jane Austen's *Persuasion*, as well as more recently *Ammonite*, about the fossil hunter, Mary Anning. From the watermill, which dates all the way back to the fourteenth century, to the beautiful St Michael's Church and the Lepers' Well, there's plenty to see and enjoy here, whatever your interests. There's a strong literary community in Lyme as well as the vibrant Marine Theatre.

"When you're on the beach, you know there is something else on the other side of the ocean. I've heard that dolphins and whales send alpha waves, healing waves. The sea is the star of the show in this town."

Chesil Beach

 Parking available

 Toilets available

 South West Coast Path

 Site of Special Scientific Interest

 Dogs allowed all year round

Scan me

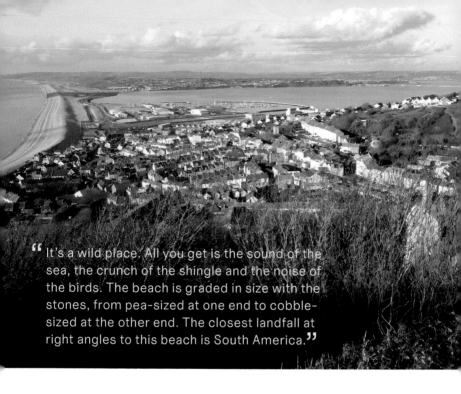

"It's a wild place. All you get is the sound of the sea, the crunch of the shingle and the noise of the birds. The beach is graded in size with the stones, from pea-sized at one end to cobble-sized at the other end. The closest landfall at right angles to this beach is South America."

This famous eighteen-mile long pebble beach stretches northwest from Portland to West Bay, separated from the mainland by the Fleet lagoon. The fleets are where smugglers would submerge their illicit goods by night as they were brought ashore, taking a stone from the beach as a marker. When returning at a safe time to retrieve the booty, the size of their stone would show them the point on the beach at which their booty was hidden. The area of shallow sand dunes overlaying shingle that points east and inward towards Portland harbour is known as Hamm Beach. Both beaches and the lagoon are in the centre of the Jurassic Coast and are part of a UNESCO World Heritage site. There's prolific wildlife here, including a tern colony in the Fleet Nature Reserve. I remember the spectacular sight of the full length of the beach including the fleets, laid out in front of me as I descended by road towards the Abbotsbury end of Chesil Beach.

"For me, the beach is a very particular kind of quiet. There isn't really a sound like it, yet at the same time you can hear sounds from a long way away as well."

Durdle Door

 Parking available   Dogs allowed all year round

 South West Coast Path   Beach cleaned regularly

 Site of Special Scientific Interest   Good water quality

Scan me

" The beach is a place
for escapism. It's a
place for relaxation. "

" The beach to me is a snapshot in time really. The beach to me means freedom, the beach to me means exploration. Every time I come down here, I find something new and something to explore. This spot is special, there's no doubt about it and that's what brings me back every single time. "

The sweeping beach at Durdle Door was once three coves until natural erosion took its toll. Durdle Door itself is one of the most photographed landmarks along the Jurassic Coast. The rock arch in the sea was formed as the softer rock was eroded away behind the hard limestone, allowing the sea to punch through them. Eventually the arch will collapse to leave a sea stack. Despite a lack of facilities, over 200,000 walkers use the path between here and Lulworth Cove, making it one of the busiest stretches on the entire South West Coast Path. I remember a bright morning visit, with clear blue sky and sea framing the limestone rock of Durdle Door and lapping against a bleached white beach. On that occasion a high vantage point, afforded by the approach from the cliffs above, also gave me a view of a recent dramatic landslide at Man o' War Bay, between here and Lulworth Cove.

Studland Bay

 Parking available

 Toilets available

 South West Coast Path

 Site of Special Scientific Interest

National Trust

Dogs allowed all year round

RNLI Lifeguard Cover (check locally)

Beach cleaned regularly

Good water quality

Scan me

> " In the summer, I like to swim in the sea, because I was born by the sea. My grandfather taught me to swim in the sea, so I always come back. It's just a terrific place. I love it. "

" I could give many reasons why Studland Beach means
so much to me. It is now just a short drive back to my
childhood home of Studland where life was spent on the
beach, exploring 'Fort Henry', beachcombing, riding my
pony along the long beach and sand dunes, swimming
in the sea from spring to autumn. Now I can sit on the
clean golden sands in summer, watching the world go
by, looking towards Old Harry Rocks to the right and
Bournemouth and beyond to the left, views imprinted in
my brain. This is a beach I will never tire of visiting. "

Made up of Knoll Beach, Middle Beach and South Beach, Studland Bay
is popular all year round, helped by its proximity to Poole and the
chain ferry across to the Isle of Purbeck. It stretches from just past the
ferry all the way round to Old Harry Rocks and includes a designated
naturist area. The wide sweeping sandy beaches are ideal for swimming,
water sports, sailing and diving. The water quality is good. Studland Bay
is of prime scientific importance for marine life, being a breeding ground
for cuttlefish and sea horses who curl their tails around the sea grass
as they graze. Once I chose South Beach for a springtime visit and was
handsomely rewarded, as the beach felt within touching distance of Old
Harry Rocks across the bay due to the clear light over the sea.

Branksome Chine

 Parking available

 Toilets available

 Bournemouth Coast Path

 Dogs allowed all year round

 RNLI Lifeguard Cover (check locally)

 Beach cleaned regularly

Scan me

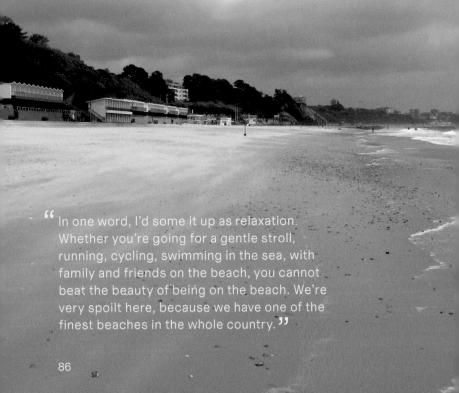

"In one word, I'd some it up as relaxation. Whether you're going for a gentle stroll, running, cycling, swimming in the sea, with family and friends on the beach, you cannot beat the beauty of being on the beach. We're very spoilt here, because we have one of the finest beaches in the whole country."

" The beach is fantastic for me. I come down whenever I can. I like to go in and have my swim. I can relax, I can get rid of all the troubles that are surrounding me and then I can sit on the beach and have a nice cup of coffee and just totally relax and warm up in the sunshine. The beach is a little place where I can come just on my own, although I have got plenty of friends down here as well. "

A chine is a wooded valley that runs down from higher ground, in this case cliffs, to the sea. There are four such chines on the long sandy beach between Poole and Bournemouth, namely Branksome, Branksome Dene, Alum and Durley. Branksome Chine has a wide sandy beach with a gradual slope into the sea, part of a seven-mile long strand of beach that runs between Poole in the west all the way to Hengistbury Head in the east. This section of beach is backed by tall cliffs that display vivid gorse in season. It's a Blue Flag beach with a beach office and lifeguard cover from May through to September. An excellent restaurant by the beach is frequented by celebrities. Although this is a well-to-do area, the beach and its views are still natural and sensational. Windsurfers can be seen riding the waves, particularly at the weekend. Other beach goers prefer a run or a walk along a promenade that is blessed with a choice of restaurants and ice cream parlours.

Mudeford Sandbank

 Parking available

 National Trust

 Toilets available

 Dogs allowed all year round

 National Nature Reserve

 Beach cleaned regularly

 Site of Special Scientific Interest

Good water quality

 Scan me

" Now we have six grandchildren and they all come down to the beach hut here. Some climb up ladders and do a little bit of work and they play about in the sand and get pretty messy. They all love it down here. That's why we keep coming back. "

" I always said I would live beside the sea at one
time and that happened. I think it is the one
thing I would really miss. It's also a very spiritual
thing. If you're feeling down, it can cheer you up.
I just love being able to come out, walk along the
beach with the sun in your face and smell the
fresh air and feel fortunate to be here. **"**

Mudeford Sandbank sits next to Hengistbury Head overlooking
Christchurch harbour and forming a natural barrier between the
harbour and the open sea. There's an adjacent lagoon where you can
see red shanks, oyster catchers, terns and natterjack toads. The area is
designated as a Site of Nature Conservation Interest and can be reached
in a variety of ways, either by foot, bicycle or land train from Hengistbury
Head, or by ferry from Mudeford and Christchurch Quays. There are about
300 beach huts on the sandbank. They are unique because you can sleep
in them overnight, so a community spirit has grown up here. There's also
a chic cafe, but the main attraction here is the work of nature, a finger of
powder fine sand in an idyllic location. Safe dinghy sailing, windsurfing and
wonderful wildlife are all to hand. There is a visitor centre by the car park. I
recommend a circular walk from this car park, taking in Hengistbury Head
itself. Try the walk on an autumn afternoon to see The Needles and the Isle
of Wight basking in the light of the lowering seasonal sun.

Hampshire and Isle of Wight, Sussex and Kent

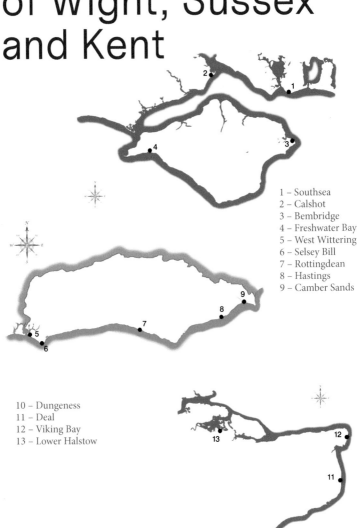

1 – Southsea
2 – Calshot
3 – Bembridge
4 – Freshwater Bay
5 – West Wittering
6 – Selsey Bill
7 – Rottingdean
8 – Hastings
9 – Camber Sands

10 – Dungeness
11 – Deal
12 – Viking Bay
13 – Lower Halstow

Southsea

 Parking available

 Toilets available

 Solent Way

 Dogs allowed (check locally)

 Beach cleaned regularly

 Good water quality

Scan me

Stretching from Southsea Castle along to Lumps Fort and beyond to Eastney, this is a long shingle beach with exposed sand at low tide. Clarence Pier is a wonderful attraction and this is definitely a family-friendly beach. There's also the Blue Reef Aquarium and the D-Day Museum to visit, along with the Pyramid Centre, which is a glass-faced leisure centre with a spa and other leisure pursuits. There's an accessible promenade behind the beach and the town is welcoming and friendly, with nearby Portsmouth also handy for visitors. Although some claim this beach is where windsurfing was invented, a striking feature for me is the Hovercraft link to Ryde on The Isle of Wight. The hovercraft has a bespoke area of beach to alight on at Southsea. With a quick turnaround, it's a speedy option for crossing to the island.

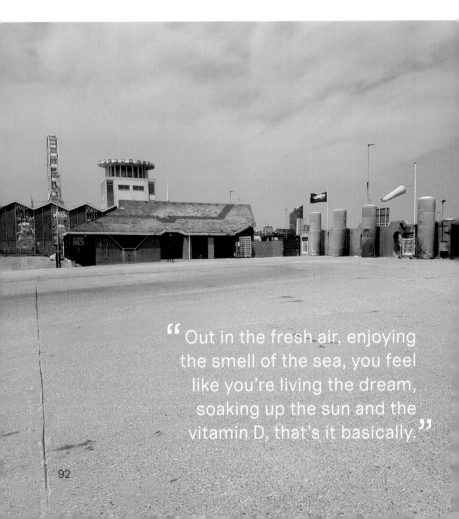

"Out in the fresh air, enjoying the smell of the sea, you feel like you're living the dream, soaking up the sun and the vitamin D, that's it basically."

" The beach for me is a really peaceful place, somewhere I can go if I'm feeling sad, somewhere calm. I think it has healing properties. Looking out to sea always brings a sense of stillness for me. It has a simplicity. We have the sand, we have the sea – it's quite simple really. "

Calshot

 Parking available

 Toilets available

 Site of Special Scientific Interest

 Dogs allowed all year round

 Beach cleaned regularly

 Good water quality

Scan me

" I love the sun. I'm a sun worshipper, so some of my happiest memories have been made on the beach. "

" I guess the main thing the beach means to me is memories. Looking back at happy times, long, lazy days at the beach in summer, watching the children grow up, but also making memories for the future as well. "

Calshot beach sits at the western end of Southampton Water where it meets The Solent. There's a handy car park and this is generally a quiet spot, ideal for watching the boats come and go to and from Southampton and out to the Isle of Wight. The beach is stony but you can walk out over sand banks at low tide. There's a nearby activity centre to visit as well. The beach is part of Calshot Spit, which itself is a one-mile long sand and shingle bank, again affording fine views. It includes a salt marsh hosting a fine diversity of wildlife, particularly birds. Another attraction here is Calshot Castle, built in 1539 by Henry VIII in a vital strategic position. The beach is clean, as is the bathing water. It's a popular spot for water sports, including sailing, kayaking, windsurfing and kitesurfing.

" I also like watching the boats, the yachts in particular. I sail as a hobby and I've done offshore racing for the last thirty-five years, mainly with JOG (Junior Outshore Group), doing mostly French ports. What do we do when we get there? Having had a beer and lunch, we head for the beach. "

Bembridge

 Parking available

 Toilets available

 Isle of Wight Costal Path

 Site of Special Scientific Interest

 Dogs allowed all year round

Beach cleaned regularly

Good water quality

 Scan me

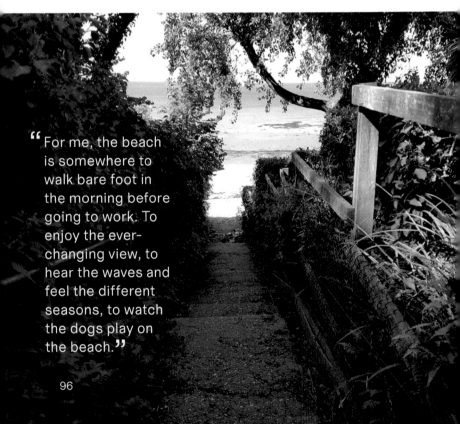

"For me, the beach is somewhere to walk bare foot in the morning before going to work. To enjoy the ever-changing view, to hear the waves and feel the different seasons, to watch the dogs play on the beach."

"The beach is just divine"

Bembridge beach runs south from the spit at the edge of the harbour. The most notable landmark is the lifeboat station, located at the end of a purpose-built 200 metres long pier. The beach is a mixture of stone and sand with interesting rock pools at low tide. Water sports are popular and there is a slipway to help with dinghy launching and recovery. As part of the eponymous Site of Special Scientific Interest, at low tide you can see Bembridge Ledge, which has snagged many an unwary sailor over the years. There is parking at each end of the beach and access is good. The village of Bembridge claims to be the biggest in England, with a population of four thousand. It sits at the most easterly point of the Isle of Wight behind the headland of Culver and even has its own airport.

" This beach is very special to us. It's a very restorative beach, a place that you come and you walk up and down and you shout your problems and you cry and you laugh. You play cricket when there is some sand and when there's not, you sit on the pebbles and you get a very sore bottom and you bring your flask and you have a cup of tea. "

Freshwater Bay

 Parking available

 Dogs allowed (check locally)

 Toilets available

 Beach cleaned regularly

 Isle of Wight Costal Path

 Good water quality

 Site of Special Scientific Interest

 Scan me

" This beach has always been very special to me. I'm 72 now and when I was 16, I came here from Bedford on a school trip. Everybody in the class loved the place. When we went back, I always had it in my heart that I wanted to go back to Freshwater Bay, because I loved it so much. **"**

The beach is set in a cove between chalky cliffs. It's a popular visitor destination with a large car park and an esplanade. Flint and pebbles adorn the beach, clattering in the waves. At low tide rock pools reveal their secrets, which are wonderful for young children. The adjacent Freshwater Marshes Site of Special Scientific Interest derives its name from the dammed-up end of the River Yar, which flows northwards to Yarmouth. There are caves which were once used by smugglers. You can explore them by kayak but take care not to be cut off by the tide. The nearby village of Freshwater is the main hub for the West of the Isle of Wight. As well as shops and a supermarket, you can visit Alfred Lord Tennyson's house, Farringdon for a house tour that celebrates the life and times of the former Poet Laureate.

" The cathartic massage of sand under the soles of your feet, the stark contrast from the built environment, the sound of nothing but the sea, all combine to make a magical medicine that can cure all ills. I love being on the beach. **"**

West Wittering

 Parking available

 Toilets available

 New Lipchis Way

 Site of Special Scientific Interest

 Dogs allowed (check locally)

 RNLI Lifeguard Cover (check locally)

 Beach cleaned regularly

Good water quality

 Scan me

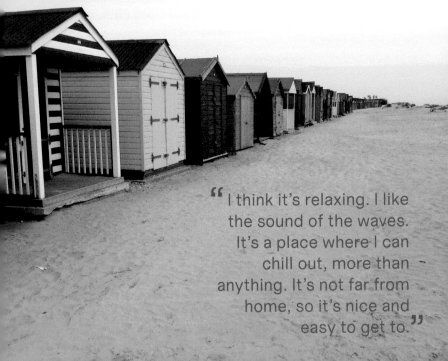

> " I think it's relaxing. I like the sound of the waves. It's a place where I can chill out, more than anything. It's not far from home, so it's nice and easy to get to. "

> " To me, the beach is where civilisation and developed places meet the wild. On the land here, it's relatively untamed, but obviously it's inhabited and it's been moulded and shaped by people, but when you look out to the sea, it's completely wild. Wherever you are, there's absolutely nothing you could do to change it. It's its own thing and it's where you can come, at any stage, to get a view of the wild. "

The most westerly of the Sussex beaches at manonabeach.com, West Wittering is also one of the most beautiful, with uncharacteristically soft sand and a fine view across The Solent to the Isle of Wight. There are picturesque sand dunes behind the beach, which is a popular escape from Chichester and further beyond. I remember on one occasion the weather was mild and dry and the tide was low enough to enjoy shell hunting in the flat, lower reaches. Another time the sun was out during an autumn visit. On a low tide with a warm breeze from the southwest, my beach walk was mild and reflective. Looking across to Hayling Island and to the Isle of Wight, I wondered at the trade in and out of Southampton over the years and the natural beauty on this side of the water.

Selsey Bill

 Parking available

 Toilets available

 Medmerry Managed Realignment Scheme

 Site of Special Scientific Interest

 Dogs allowed (check locally)

Beach cleaned regularly

Scan me

❝ This is a working beach, fifty-three years of fishing for me.
I used to go with my father before I left school in the spring
to row, because you couldn't use an engine in those days,
to catch prawns before they vanished again into deeper
water. The big boats used to carry a pair of oars and sails.
My father's big boat was 28 foot, a ship's lifeboat. She had
a Kelvin engine in her and she was petrol and paraffin. ❞

Inshore boats still bring whelks, crab and lobster ashore at Selsey
Bill. Traceable generations of the family of Norman James Woodland
have been fishing at Selsey Bill for 932 years, an unbroken chain that
is also claimed by other families. Due to the treacherous nature of the
sea around the Bill, there is also a lifeboat stationed here. The western
shoreline at Selsey Bill is protected and managed in two ways, with
the West Sands Coastal Protection Scheme guarding the beach at the
Holiday Park and the Medmerry Managed Realignment Scheme run by
the Environment Agency, which has a policy of managed retreat in the
face of the sea. That beach is on Manhood Peninsula, the most southerly
tip of West Sussex. My visit was to the eastern beach.

❝ Fishing took my interest at a young age and has done ever
since. Now, in my mid-fifties, it's getting harder, but I still
love the job. You are your own boss. We have small boats
on the beach and we use them to get off to the larger
ones offshore. Sometimes, it's not too easy getting off,
on days when it's rough on the shore. On days when it's
lovely and calm, you couldn't have a better job. ❞

Rottingdean

 Parking available

 Toilets available

 Site of Special Scientific Interest

 Dogs allowed (check locally)

 Scan me

" For me, it's very relaxing. I've been living by the beach for the last forty years. It's always different. The colours are different. It's good exercise too."

"It's so beautiful along here, this whole stretch, that I just feel I have to make use of it. I think it does me good, in terms of tranquillity and putting my life back into some kind of perspective. I moved down here ten years ago and it's the best thing I ever did. It's beauty, it's wildness, it's serene in my ways, although it's wild and it's just makes my life complete."

Picturesque Rottingdean lies off the busy tourist trail. It's a small, picture-perfect town with a historic past and a friendly welcome. The main features in the town are Kipling's Garden, Rottingdean Windmill and St. Margaret's Church, with its beautiful stained glass windows. There are some traditional old inns which were once frequented by smugglers in the area due to the remoteness of the town and its proximity to the sea. These times are referenced in Kipling's "A Smuggler's Song":

"Five and twenty ponies
Trotting through the dark
Brandy for the Parson
Baccy for the Clerk."

The beach itself is relatively secluded and backed by strikingly high chalk cliffs. Rottingdean has its own micro-climate. Facing south and in the lee of cool northerly breezes, the high white cliffs reflect and radiate the sun onto the beach and the promenade below. I remember one visit when the tide was high, the waves were wild and the winter sun was bright in the sky. The stylish performance stage near the beach pays respect to the folk singing Copper family from Rottingdean. It makes you want to linger here in the hope of a tune. Out beyond the beach at low tide are white chalk pavements formed by the erosion that is a permanent feature of this part of the coast.

Hastings

 Parking available

 Toilets available

 Site of Special Scientific Interest

 Dogs allowed (check locally)

 RNLI Lifeguard Cover (check locally)

 Beach cleaned regularly

 Good water quality

Scan me

" It means everything. It's family related. Me and my brother over there, we have been doing it (fishing) since we were nippers. It's in your blood. It's in your veins. "

PROGRESS

Pelham is the main beach in Hastings, facing southeast and made largely of shingle. Much of this beach has been created from land reclaimed from the sea. With the advent of the railways in the nineteenth century, more tourists arrived in Hastings, requiring greater beach space. As well as being a popular visitor attraction due to its proximity to Battle, as in the Battle of Hastings, this is the main Cinque Port in East Sussex. It enjoys both a proud Royal Charter and has a strong fishing tradition, including a healthy, thriving Sea Angling Association. The inshore fishing fleet lands a varied catch; on one of my visits, the Senlac Jack brought home cuttlefish and some Dover sole. On their return from the sea, boats of up to eighteen tons are hauled up the beach by caterpillar tractors.

" It's our working environment. We work from the open beach. We are commercial fishermen. It's a very old fleet. We have been here over a thousand years and some families date back that far, so the beach is where we are working, day-to-day. The rights of the open beach for the fishermen here are from a charter from when they were conscripted and fought against The Spanish Armada.**"**

Camber Sands

 Parking available

 Toilets available

 Dogs allowed (check locally)

 Beach cleaned regularly

 Good water quality

 Scan me

" It means friendship, happiness and tranquillity. "

" The beach is freedom, equality for all. We can
come out in any weather. The sea is always
breathtaking, whether it's a calm, still day with
beautiful skies or a bit like this, when it's the
winter, the waves are rolling in and we're here
free, flying with our thoughts and our dreams,
taking in the fresh air and it's all for free. **"**

Camber Sands is a popular sandy beach with picturesque dunes and interesting wildlife, located near the village of Camber. The marram grass that you see covering much of the dunes has a deep root system which helps to hold the sand in place. Traditional chestnut fences help sand to build up more quickly. It's this combination of plants and fences that prevents the dunes from moving and burying the village. There is plenty of wildlife and vegetation to see, including the brown-tail moth caterpillar, skylarks, sea spurge and the lethal berries of the black nightshade. I remember one visit on a full tide with the sea running right up against the dunes, seething with energy. Another visit during the summer brought a low tide, with warm weather and bright skies to complement the natural arc of the bay, which is flat and sandy. Sometimes there's a harmony among people that you can feel palpably in a natural environment and this was such an occasion.

Dungeness

 Parking available

 Toilets available

 Site of Special Scientific Interest

 Dogs allowed all year round

 Scan me

"I like how calm it is at the beach, very tranquil."

❝ I love the openness of it. I love the sounds, the birds, the seagulls; I love the pebbles and all the different grasses; and then the sea itself, all the different colours in the sea and the contrast with the sky. Here, as well, we have the sound of the Dymchurch Railway and this particular beach is unique, very different from other beaches, it's very special. **❞**

Technically classified as the UK's only desert, Dungeness beach is the second largest shingle formation in the world. It's a wildlife paradise featuring bats, stoats, marsh frogs, varied birdlife and several RSPB hides, as well as 600 species of plants and rare insects. There's a public car park or you can arrive by steam train from Hythe, using the Romney, Hythe and Dymchurch Railway. The "patch" or "boil" is a favourite angling spot and bathing isn't recommended, so this is first and foremost a wildlife destination. Dogs are allowed and there's a lighthouse, a couple of pubs, fish 'n chips, plus a plethora of characterful beach shacks, including filmmaker Derek Jarman's Prospect Cottage. I recommend a visit to The Old Lighthouse, commissioned in 1904 and de-commissioned in 1960. Standing forty-six metres high, the internal mezzanine slate floors and their steel beams are particularly impressive.

❝ For me, it's very good for the soul and you can come here and breathe the lovely clean air. Every now and then, as the train goes past, you get a lovely smell of the steam from the train coming. It feels very clean here and something about it makes my soul sing. **❞**

Deal

 Parking available

 Toilets available

 Dogs allowed (check locally)

 Beach cleaned regularly

 Good water quality

Scan me

> " I'm originally from London and I've always wanted to live by the sea. When I retired, I moved to Deal to be by the sea. There's just something about the beach, whether it's stones or the sand is irrelevant, I just seem to be closer to nature and that's about it. "

This is a long shingle beach that runs from north of Kingsdown beach past Walmer beach to the town of Deal with its pier, a popular spot for fishing. It is a dog-friendly beach and there are wonderful walks in both directions from Deal. The promenade behind the beach, with smartly presented beach huts, gives an upmarket feel to any visit. The town itself has many independent shops and businesses. It's also steeped in history, with a Tudor castle and a Conservation Area encompassing part of the town. There is a slipway for sailing boats and leisure craft. Sea fishing, sailing and swimming in the clean bathing water are also popular.

> " I love my visits to Deal. I can be down here in no time from London for some much-needed rest and recuperation. When I wake up near to the beach, from my window I hear the pebbles rolling in the sea and smell the fresh air, then out for a walk and breakfast at a local cafe. It's all I need and puts me back in my stride. "

113

Viking Bay

 Parking available

 RNLI Lifeguard Cover (check locally)

 Toilets available

 Beach cleaned regularly

 Site of Special Scientific Interest

 Good water quality

 Dogs allowed (check locally)

Scan me

"This is the top corner of Kent and I like the view from the top of the cliff. I have a coffee here every morning. The gardens are clean and tidy. It's a nice place. It'll do for me."

"Yes, it's a beautiful place."

"It's a beautiful beach and it has a lot of history. It means a lot to a lot of families, who come back to the same chalets every year for generations. In different seasons, the visitors change like the tide, like an ebb and flow of people."

Broadstairs is a quintessential seaside town, with a crescent-shaped beach at Viking Bay and to the north of the beach a quaint harbour with fishing boats. The town is well-to-do and has all the facilities that you'll need. History is all around you, for example Bleak House, where Charles Dickens wrote David Copperfield. There is lifeguard cover in the summer and the bathing water is clean. Down on the beach, below the striking white cliffs, you'll find children's rides and characterful beach huts. To top off the setting there is a cliff-side elevator at the southern end of the beach to save any weary legs from the walk up to town. Viking Bay is highly diverse in its attractions and it is the smartest of the beaches in and around Broadstairs.

115

Lower Halstow

 Parking available

 Toilets available

 Dogs allowed all year round

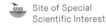 Site of Special Scientific Interest

 Scan me

> **"** Somewhere to enjoy a good walk in a good atmosphere with the sound of the sea breaking, in some cases just to enjoy the solitude. **"**

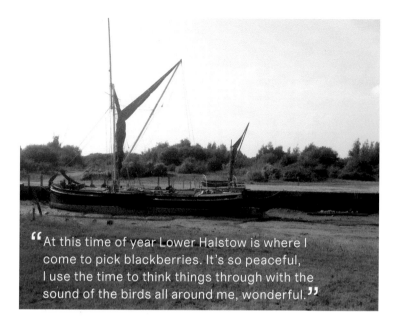

" At this time of year Lower Halstow is where I come to pick blackberries. It's so peaceful, I use the time to think things through with the sound of the birds all around me, wonderful. "

Tucked away in the recesses of the River Medway, Lower Halstow is predominantly a leisure sailing venue. It has its own yacht club. There are visitor moorings, but these only offer sufficient depth for an hour and a half either side of high tide. The location is stunning with fruit trees next to the creek. The tidal mudflats attract wading birds, including oystercatchers, turnstones and black-headed gulls. The village features the charming church of St Margaret of Antioch, which dates back to Saxon times in the eighth century and features later additions such as the thirteenth-century tower. Lower Halstow is also a popular location for filmmakers. Credits include the Hollywood blockbuster Wonder Woman, with scenes filmed at the wharf.

Norfolk and Suffolk

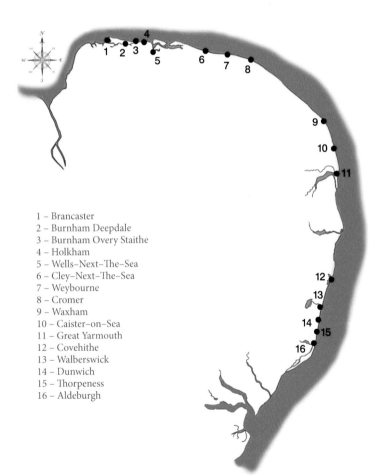

1 – Brancaster
2 – Burnham Deepdale
3 – Burnham Overy Staithe
4 – Holkham
5 – Wells–Next–The–Sea
6 – Cley–Next–The–Sea
7 – Weybourne
8 – Cromer
9 – Waxham
10 – Caister–on–Sea
11 – Great Yarmouth
12 – Covehithe
13 – Walberswick
14 – Dunwich
15 – Thorpeness
16 – Aldeburgh

Brancaster

 Parking available

 Site of Special Scientific Interest

 Toilets available

 Nature Reserve

 Norfolk Coast Path

 Dogs allowed all year round

Scan me

Brancaster has a stunning beach, stretching for miles in front of a golf course and sand dunes. At low tide you can see the wreck of the SS Vina. The soft sand is ideal for making sandcastles and on windy days it's an ideal spot for kite surfing. There are excellent shops, restaurants and boat trips running from Brancaster Staithe. Birdlife, both resident and migratory, features strongly along this stretch of coastline, including marsh harriers, avocets, oystercatchers and terns. Brancaster is known for its mussels, in season when there is an 'R' in the month. I remember on one occasion a low tide coinciding with cold, clear skies that reflected light from the myriad razor clam shells scattered on the expansive, flat beach. The azure blue skies provided a counterpoint to the rich, recently washed sand. The sense of scale and perspective here can be mesmerising and uplifting at the same time. Take care close to the sea as the tide turns back in, as it returns swiftly to its high water mark. This beach is elemental. As the razor clam shells crunch underfoot, there is a time for contemplation, creativity, re-balancing or just fun, whichever sense guides you.

> " For me, it's the beginning of the sea, the beginning of another world. It's the beginning of some other life, a life that you can't see just here. You can imagine some legend in the sea. It's amazing for me. "

" It's peace really, more than anything else. This particular beach is different every day. It stimulates the senses, while giving you that peacefulness. You can just ease down and it's worth it. You can keep going for years, I hope. "

Burnham Deepdale

 Parking available

 Norfolk Coast Path

 Dogs allowed all year round

 Scan me

"As you can see, I'm coming to a wild and remote area. We can walk all morning and hardly see anybody."

122

Burnham Deepdale is a tranquil and remote part of the Burnhams. Located next to the village of Brancaster, it lies among the creeks and marshes inside Brancaster Harbour. The sea wall stretches a mile inland to accommodate the tide, with salt marshes to one side and freshwater meadows to the other, affording an outstanding view. This is a fascinating area, steeped in history, with Nelson's birthplace, Burnham Thorpe, nearby along with the Holkham Estate. For one afternoon visit in winter, with a pale sun shedding some light through the intense, stormy sky over Burnham Deepdale, the fragile scale of the sea wall gave this setting a frontier feel, although the tide was out and the sea felt miles away. The greys, browns, blacks and blues of the land melded into the sky, so the environment seemed almost spherical, as if one was standing on a thin ribbon of land in the middle of it all. On another occasion, walking along the sea wall towards Scolt Head Island, I saw a couple of egrets and a redshank. The sounds of nature resonated and there was a clear view across the salt marsh towards the sea. This is a birdwatcher's paradise and the walk leads to the wonderful beaches at Holkham and Wells-Next-The-Sea.

" I have a particular interest in art and I always find that going to the sea again, the call of the wild, in effect, it brings you back to the scene used by nineteenth-century artists like Stanhope Forbes from Cornwall in Newlyn. Artists flocked around there, because they identified the wonderful light, the beautiful sunshine, capturing that one particular moment. I think of artists like Alfred Munnings. He loved all of this area and coming back to his home ground on the East Anglian coast. "

Burnham Overy Staithe

 Parking available

 Toilets available

 Norfolk Coast Path

 Dogs allowed all year round

Scan me

" Peace, tranquillity, space and the sky, the sea. It's just awe-inspiring and no two days are the same. The beach looks different every day, the way the water lies, the distance of the tide, how strong the current is and what's washed up on the shore. I couldn't live without it. "

> " The whole area feels like an unspoilt refuge; it's a place to breathe, unwind, and let go. "

> " What we call 'the beach' is actually the island called Scolt Head; you can walk there at low tide, or you can take one of the ferries as the tide comes in. The beach is completely unspoilt, and there are plenty of people both sailing and swimming in what is known as 'the lagoon', between the land and the island. There is also another 'beach' close by called 'Bank Hole'; even at the lowest tide you can swim here, and apparently there's a freshwater spring at the bottom of the hole. This is the ideal place to drop out of life for a while. "

The Burnhams are considered by many to be the jewel in the crown of North Norfolk. Burnham Overy Staithe is a haven for sailing enthusiasts and is a characterful place. A channel leads to the sea. A bracing walk takes visitors out to an unspoilt beach, which itself links to Holkham and Wells-Next-The-Sea beaches further along the coast. Take care with the tides on this walk, though, to avoid being cut off. The path is flat, as you would expect, and you should reach the beach in less than half an hour. It is well worth it as it is completely unspoilt and backed by dunes. I was struck by the sheer scale and size of the sky and the scudding white clouds.

Holkham

 Parking available

 Toilets available

 Norfolk Coast Path & Peddars Way

 Site of Special Scientific Interest

 Dogs allowed all year round

Scan me

" This beach has come from my childhood, really. We used to play cricket on the beach and all sorts of things, pirate adventures. Here we are, 45 years later, it's just the open space and the feeling of freedom here, a fabulous place to be. "

This is the most well-known North Norfolk beach, with miles of natural beauty and a great sense of space. As part of the Holkham Estate, the beach is usually accessed via Lady Anne's Drive opposite the Victoria Inn. There is a variety of walks. A left turn at the bottom of the drive takes you through the pinewoods and back along the beach. Turning right takes you towards Wells-Next-The-Sea and its lifeboat house and dunes. This beach has remarkable light and it's no wonder that it has featured in many films, including the final scene of "Shakespeare in Love". Holkham is a spectacular beach to visit at any time. Horses exercise along the shoreline. I remember a dense bed of razor clam shells whistling musically in the breeze as I walked towards the tree-lined backdrop to this stunning beach. I recommend an early morning visit to gain a few moments alone with your thoughts. This is a special place.

" I love this beach. I come down here every day, whatever the weather, rain, snow, blow. When I come down here, it clears your mind and you think of nothing. When there's just me and the dog on the beach, it's just fantastic, no-one else around except just me, sea, sand and sky. "

Wells-Next-The-Sea

 Parking available

 Toilets available

 Norfolk Coast Path

 Dogs allowed (check locally)

 RNLI Lifeguard Cover (check locally)

 Beach cleaned regularly

 Good water quality

 Scan me

" The beach means to me family and fun and sandcastles and being relaxed. "

The sandy beach at Wells, backed by dunes and pine trees, is part of the Holkham Estate and leads round to Holkham beach. It stretches for miles to the west into Holkham Bay. Eastwards, the beach continues but can be cut off by the tide. In this direction are salt marshes, which are part of a nature reserve. Sprats and whelks are the local speciality here. During the summer you can take a miniature railway from the town to the beach. The beach is beautiful and has formed the backdrop for many films. The sense of space is breathtaking. If you stand on the established dunes in the middle, the panorama takes in beach huts, with Wells Woods behind and an apparently endless vista out to sea across the river channel. This is kept clear for the boats that take workers out to service the offshore wind farm.

" It's like heaven. The skies are so big and the seascape is so wide. When I was young the tide used to come under these beach huts twice a day. The dunes have all grown up since I was a child. Most years, I come here with my family, often several times. **"**

Cley-Next-The-Sea

 Parking available

 Toilets available

 Norfolk Coast Path

 Dogs allowed all year round

Scan me

" I enjoy coming down here for fishing, for bass, dabs and there might be the odd mackerel. Cod or whiting can come in. It's nice to come down and try to catch some fish. "

Pronounced "Cly", Cley-Next-The-Sea is located in an Area of Outstanding Natural Beauty between Blakeney and Holt on the main coast road between Wells-Next-The-Sea and Sheringham. The Norfolk Coastal Path passes this way. The scenery here is outstanding and the area is also popular with sea anglers. The beach itself is sparse and unspoilt, with the odd fishing boat pulled up on the higher reaches of the steep shingle beach. It's a favourite with birdwatchers, who come to enjoy the migratory and resident birds. For a walk, I recommend the long stretch north to Blakeney Point. I remember the overcast sky, fused into the horizon, with the brightly coloured pebbles and shells providing a visual counterpoint. The mood was laconic and slightly wistful. On another visit, a redshank could be seen on a post top on the approach road. Behind the beach, the village of Cley-Next-The-Sea features independent food shops, including an excellent smokehouse and pretty, indigenous flint cottages.

" This beach means holiday to me. Beaches in general make me quite happy. They are a peaceful place and a fun place. I always have a good time on beaches. I like them. "

Weybourne

 Parking available

 Norfolk Coast Path

 Dogs allowed all year round

 Scan me

> " It's a place apart from the rest of my life. You can be transgressive, so it's a place I can come and be a slightly different part of myself. It's a bit like singing or dancing, you can come and be the bits that you aren't the rest of the time. "

Weybourne is an old fishing village with a rich history. It's a stopping point on the North Norfolk Railway, as well as hosting the Muckleburgh Collection of tanks. The beach is a mixture of shingle and sand. Like Cley-Next-The-Sea and Salthouse to the west, the beach is popular with sea anglers. The village of Weybourne is picturesque, with a fine fifteenth-century church and the ruins of an Augustinian priory. The windmill landmark guides you there. Muckleburgh Hill and Kelling Heath offer outstanding scenery and wildlife. The soft cliffs by the beach are modest in size but they appear striking when set in this low-lying environment. A salt marsh behind the shingle beach attracts migratory birds. There's a fine 360° view from the top of the cliffs, which forms part of the coast path here. On one visit I noticed a couple of sea swimmers enjoying the bright sunshine on a tranquil summer day.

> " It means the division between land and sea. The constant movement suggests that there is always change. It can be rough, but on the whole it's gentle, it's soothing, it's quite calming to walk along it and there's a continuum about it. There's always something happening there. "

Cromer

 Parking available

 Toilets available

Norfolk Coast Path

Dogs allowed (check locally)

 RNLI Lifeguard Cover (check locally)

 Beach cleaned regularly

 Good water quality

Scan me

" Look at that view, with the sound of the waves in the background. You can't really beat it, to be honest. "

" Cromer is somewhere I think I've been into since I was a
little girl. I've lived away from Norfolk for large chunks of
my life and come back, as people often do, for the calm
and the quiet and the air. It's somewhere to think and I
just feel very at home here. I've been to a lot of places in
the world and still Cromer is very beautiful to me. **"**

Cromer was popularised in Victorian times and remains a combination
of the old and the new. The historic seafront has guest houses that
date back to the late 1800s. Landscaped cliff gardens, which bloom with
colour during the summer months, overlook vast stretches of unspoilt,
sandy beach. A small funfair near the town is ideal for young children,
while all ages will enjoy crabbing, a pastime keenly pursued along the
spectacular pier. The narrow streets are filled with interesting shops
and plenty of places to enjoy the excellent food, including the famous
Cromer crab. You can have your crab boiled and dressed in Cromer and
enjoy it while sitting by the pier. I remember the crowds of visitors on a
summer visit; families played on the golden sands and people thronged
the characterful streets.

Waxham

 Norfolk Coast Path

 Dogs allowed all year round

Scan me

"It means being very small and having a big beach all to myself. I remember in the 1940s, nobody was on the beach and I used to just walk into the sea, paddle around and go home. Sometimes there was nobody in sight."

Located just south of Sea Palling, Waxham Sands, as it's also known at the southern end, falls within the Norfolk Coast Area of Outstanding Natural Beauty. Like Horsey Gap, this is a great location for seal-spotting, particularly in the winter, when grey seals come ashore to give birth. The white pups are fed by their mothers for three weeks on the beach. The sandy and isolated beach is a joy to walk on. Looking north, you can see the sea reefs at Sea Palling, with Horsey visible well to the south. As far as activities are concerned, this is a safe place for swimming, kayaking and occasionally surfing. If you're after peace and tranquillity in an exquisite natural setting, this is the beach for you, a Norfolk gem.

"I always associate it with being on holiday. It's being relaxed, different moods, different colours, watching the birds, different types of sand, different sounds, looking for gannets and terns and curlew, just chilling out, listening to the noises and looking for nice stones and shells, reading my book and feeling very calm."

Caister-on-Sea

 Parking available

 Dogs allowed all year round

 Toilets available

 Beach cleaned regularly

 Norfolk Coast Path

 Good water quality

Scan me

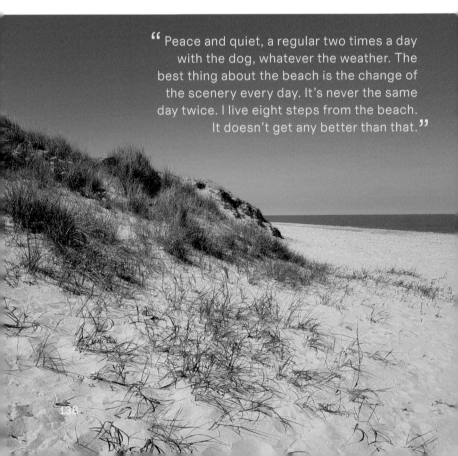

" Peace and quiet, a regular two times a day with the dog, whatever the weather. The best thing about the beach is the change of the scenery every day. It's never the same day twice. I live eight steps from the beach. It doesn't get any better than that. "

Located just to the north of Great Yarmouth, the beach at Caister-on-Sea is quieter than its popular neighbour. It's a fine dog-walking spot, with no restrictions and access is good. There is a visitor centre. Caister is proud of its independent lifeboat station, responsible for saving many lives at sea. Out at sea is Scroby Sands Wind Farm, one of many on the east coast of Britain. The thirty turbines are a sign of the times, as we switch to more renewable sources of energy. Bathing is safe and the water is clean. I recommend this long beach for a leisurely stroll, keeping a look out for seals from the colony further up the coast.

" The phrase 'Caister men never come back' is from the 1901 disaster. Trying to launch the lifeboat, it overturned and nine crew lost their lives. They had an inquest and the coxswain was asked if he was returning at the time. He said 'We would never turn back' and the phrase was changed to 'Caister men never turn back', which we never do. "

Great Yarmouth

 Parking available

 Toilets available

 Norfolk Coast Path

 Dogs allowed (check locally)

 RNLI Lifeguard Cover (check locally)

 Beach cleaned regularly

Scan me

"It means visiting old memories of when you were a child, with people you knew who have passed. You can go to all these fancy places around the world, but they don't bring back the memories. And that's it."

" The beach in Great Yarmouth means everything to me. I've been on the beach since I was a toddler. I'm now 67 years old and I still come down twice a day, particularly with the dog. My father used to take me to the beach. In fact the morning when he died, I was standing on the beach and a seagull came and sat at the side of me and that was my father. "

Great Yarmouth is Norfolk's most popular resort. The length of the beach means that you can always find a secluded spot or choose to mix with the crowds of holidaymakers. Yarmouth is loud, bright and brash. There's plenty of action to enjoy in the town, with diverse shops and a vibrant nightlife. On one of my visits it was a bright and breezy summer day. The rides were in full flow on the promenade and the pier was packed with visitors. A low tide gave access to the acres of golden sand by the Britannia Pier. There is everything to hand in nearby Great Yarmouth, yet the town beach feels unspoilt. If you want more privacy try South Beach, located between the pier and the outer harbour at the mouth of the River Yare.

141

Covehithe

 Suffolk Coast Path

 Nature Reserve

 Dogs allowed
(check locally)

SSSI Site of Special Scientific Interest

Scan me

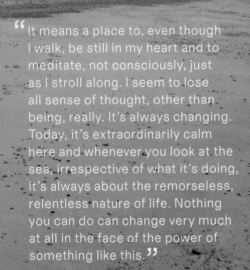

"It means a place to, even though I walk, be still in my heart and to meditate, not consciously, just as I stroll along. I seem to lose all sense of thought, other than being, really. It's always changing. Today, it's extraordinarily calm here and whenever you look at the sea, irrespective of what it's doing, it's always about the remorseless, relentless nature of life. Nothing you can do can change very much at all in the face of the power of something like this."

142

The outstanding natural beauty at Covehithe beach is discovered after a pleasant walk from the ruins of the church. On one occasion barley was ripening in the adjacent fields as I approached the beach, which sits in front of a nature reserve, itself located just behind the dunes. There are also fine walks down to Dunwich Heath and Minsmere Reserve. The beach is flat, sandy and backed by small cliffs that are being quickly eroded. This is a very tranquil and invigorating spot, with the reed beds and waterways of the nature reserve nearby. The beach has soft, crumbling cliffs and these are a magnet for birdwatchers, geologists and fossil-hunters. Echinoids and corals can be found here, along with evidence of the geological formation Norwich Crag. There's an elemental feel at Covehithe, where the land, the sea and the sky meet.

"It's a chance for me to recharge my batteries."

Walberswick

 Parking available

 Toilets available

 Suffolk Coast Path

 Nature Reserve

 Site of Special Scientific Interest

 Dogs allowed
(check locally)

  Scan me

" The beach means sort of everything. I have to come to the sea every day, sometimes up to five times a day in the summer. It's so spacious. It lifts you, as you come over the bank and suddenly, it's all open under the sky, really beautiful **"**

" I can't be away from it. Whenever I have to go away somewhere, I get withdrawal symptoms. I can hear it when I get home. I have my window open all through the year, so I can hear the sea. The sea goes with the Suffolk sky. The skies are so beautiful, especially here in Walberswick. It's a wonderful environment to live in. "

Walberswick sits on the south bank of the River Blyth, across from Southwold. The location is idyllic, attracting visitors throughout the year. The usual approach to the beach is via a small wooden bridge, lending a sense of theatre as it leads you over a hill made by the dunes and onwards down to the sea and the sandy beach. There is plenty of crabbing for children on the pier. All in all, Walberswick is a great destination, either for a family day out at the seaside or for moorland walks nearby. I remember one visit particularly. A stiff, mild breeze was the order of the day. Clouds scudded across the wide open sky, as the relentless sea rattled the shingle on the beach. The vibrant and invigorating atmosphere created a natural cauldron of sights and sounds, with gulls pitching on the breeze and the grass of the dunes bending with the wind. To step out from the shelter of one of the many beach huts is to enter a sensory maelstrom, wonderful in its detachment from everyday concerns. If you are here in the early evening light, look along to the Blyth from the sand dunes above the beach. You will see long shadows, casting a languid perspective on the shingle and sandy beach.

Dunwich

 Parking available

 Toilets available

 Suffolk Coast Path

 Site of Special Scientific Interest

 Dogs allowed all year round

 Scan me

" For me, the beach is about reflection and, being an introvert, I do a lot of reflecting. You can reflect on the whole span of life, so thinking as a child wandering along the beach throwing stones, looking out and seeing what feels like eternity. You can reflect on the entire span of existence and I love that about the beach. "

Dunwich and Dunwich Heath, which extends back from the cliffs by the beach, offer unspoilt beauty and the chance to get back to nature. There's a smuggling tradition here and plenty of history, as witnessed by the remains of Leiston Abbey, the imposing walls of Framlingham Castle and the beautifully preserved keep at Orford Castle. On one winter visit, a cold, still mist entranced the beach goers. The opaque light of the winter sun in the south moved fleetingly across the calm sea, as children searched for hag stones on the shore. A hag stone is a stone with a hole in the middle, bored out over time by the action of another wedged companion stone. Keep one with you to ward off witches, according to folklore.

" I can't go a year without coming down here all the way from South Yorkshire to Suffolk, just to recharge my batteries, just to touch the place again and feel it again, to feel good and to feel renewed to go back again. "

Thorpeness

 Parking available

 Toilets available

 Suffolk Coast Path

 Dogs allowed
(check locally)

Scan me

" Whenever I'm at the beach in Suffolk, it feels like I'm coming home. The beach takes me back in history, because it's the waves constantly coming. We are an island race, after all, so it must hold a dear part in all of us, I think."

Located just north of Aldeburgh, Thorpeness is a fascinating seaside village with brightly coloured mock Tudor style buildings. The beach is mainly sandy, and behind the village is a myriad of footpaths over the heath and common land. It has associations with J M Barrie's Peter Pan and an appropriately whimsical ambience. Rod fishermen work from the beach and there is always plenty of room for a good stroll along the shingle. In the near distance to the south, the mist can make neighbouring Aldeburgh appear as a faraway land despite its proximity. An attraction is The House in the Clouds, sitting on top of an old water tower. Available as a holiday let, it sits behind the lake, which is known as The Mere.

"All sorts of different memories, most of them happy, some funny, some a little bit sad. My children growing up, my parents skinny-dipping. Now I see my great nephews and nieces on it and it's never the same. It's always changing and it's just as lovely in the winter as it is in the summer."

Aldeburgh

 Parking available

 Toilets available

 Suffolk Coast Path

 Dogs allowed
(check locally)

Scan me

> " To me, it means smoked fish. The fish is landed on the beach and we smoke it in our hut here. Most of the fish we smoke is supplied locally. The favourites are the local sprats and kippers, the herring generally. The beach to me is where my livelihood comes from; you can't beat it. "

The beach at Aldeburgh is a wonderful place to be on a misty, still winter morning. The sea's music on the shingle is the only sound, just before the town wakes up and the early boats return with their catches. The pebbles have been endlessly turned upon and between each other, becoming smooth to the touch and harmoniously coloured. On mornings like these it's hard to pick out the horizon as the massive sky folds into the sea. The mist seems to amplify each small sound, yet the intimacy remains. Weekends entice a throng of visitors to the pretty streets and to the independent shops, all a stone's throw from the shingle beach and its fresh fish vendors. On one occasion I witnessed the making of a commissioned film about Benjamin Britten and his affinity to Aldeburgh, a reflection on the perennial relationship between man and place – Benjamin Britten Centenary Film. Aldeburgh also counts artist Maggi Hambling among its luminaries and you can see her shell sculpture on the beach towards Thorpeness.

“ Aldeburgh beach, to me, means a British beach. It's stony, the sea can look very grey sometimes, as well as looking beautifully blue. The sky goes for ever here and the light is just very special. You can see Aldeburgh beach coming for quite a way, when you're making your way towards it.”

North of England

1 – Beadnell Bay
2 – Bamburgh
3 – Seahouses
4 – Alnmouth
5 – Runswick Bay
6 – Hunmanby Gap
7 – Fraisthorpe

8 – Ainsdale–on–Sea
9 – Crosby
10 – Hoylake Red Rocks

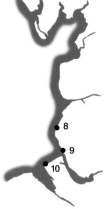

Beadnell Bay

 Parking available

 Toilets available

 Northumberland Coast Path

 Site of Special Scientific Interest

 National Trust

 Dogs allowed all year round

 Good water quality

 Scan me

Beadnell Bay features a sandy beach, backed by the dunes of Newton Links. It runs from the village of Beadnell to Snook Point in the south. Curiously, the village of Beadnell features a west-facing harbour. Boats leave the harbour in the direction of the beach before turning out to sea. The westerly aspect enables visitors to enjoy the sunset while looking over the beach. This is part of the Northumberland Coast Area of Outstanding Natural Beauty on the Northumberland Heritage Coast. Water sports are popular here, particularly windsurfing, canoeing and kitesurfing, as there's plenty of sand on the flat beach. You can take a boat trip from here to the nearby Farne Islands, where you will see puffins, terns and seals. Finally, there's a welcoming fifteenth-century pub within striking distance of the beach.

" With a west-facing harbour located on the east coast, there is both character and beauty at Beadnell Bay. This beach for me is ever-changing, a great place to unwind and a great place for a walk at any time in an exceptional natural environment. **"**

" Great Great Great Grandfather, he was an agricultural worker who came down from the West and was farming on the coast. He married a fisherman's daughter. That's how the Dixons got into fishing at Beadnell Bay in the late 1800s. By 1900, there were eight Dixon fishermen in Beadnell. I'm retired but I'm the last one. "

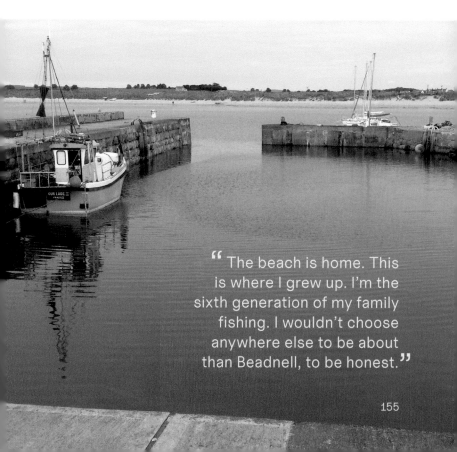

" The beach is home. This is where I grew up. I'm the sixth generation of my family fishing. I wouldn't choose anywhere else to be about than Beadnell, to be honest. "

155

Bamburgh

 Parking available

 Toilets available

 Northumberland Coast Path

 Farne Islands

 Site of Special Scientific Interest

 Dogs allowed all year round

 Good water quality

 Scan me

" The beach to me means happiness. It evokes memories of childhood holidays, running through the sand with that fresh, salty breeze, the clean air, the crashing of the waves, escapism. It gets you away from everything. "

A candidate for "best beach in England" in many surveys, this is a white, sandy beach, featuring Bamburgh Castle as a backdrop beyond the dunes. The nearby town of Bamburgh has a well-to-do feel. Holy Island at Lindisfarne is visible to the north. The Farne Islands are a haven for seals, puffins and terns. There are no fewer than three designated Sites of Special Scientific Interest here – Bamburgh Coast and Hills, Bamburgh Dunes and Northumberland Shore. The expansive nature of the beach makes it popular with dog walkers and horse riders. I recommend a walk to the north past Bamburgh Castle to beautiful Budle Bay. If you head south to Seahouses instead, there is a bus back to save your legs.

"Bamburgh is special in so many ways. From the castle with its history to the Farne Islands with its wildlife, from the sandy beach to the nature here, it keeps me coming back and it always will."

Seahouses

 Parking available

 Toilets available

 Northumberland Coast Path

 Farne Islands

 Site of Special Scientific Interest

 Dogs allowed all year round

 Good water quality

Scan me

"Take a trip to the Farne Islands on a boat from Seahouses, you won't regret it. Then a tub of prawns on the quayside, perfect."

158

" The beach means to me big open spaces, wilderness, looking out to sea. I'm a massive nature lover, so going to see wildlife, spending time with the family and appreciating weather. "

The village of Seahouses sits between two beaches. Seahouses North is a sandy beach with European designated bathing water. It lies just above a historic fishing village, with its small harbour; this is the usual departure point for boat trips out to the Farne Islands. Seahouses South, commonly known as Annstead, features abundant rock pools to be explored when the tide falls away. This beach is backed by dunes and is part of a local nature reserve. Both beaches are well served by the village. It is a popular spot for sea anglers. The village is a hub for Northumberland tourism, due to its proximity to such beautiful beaches and the great seafood on offer, not least excellent fish and chips.

Alnmouth

 Parking available

 Toilets available

 Northumberland Coast Path

 Site of Special Scientific Interest

 Dogs allowed all year round

Beach cleaned regularly

Scan me

"It's about family and relaxing and sea and peace."

"The beach means a bit of escape from the day-to-day, some time off work and some time with the family, not really thing about much, other than sandcastles."

Alnmouth is the local beach for nearby Alnwick, itself well worth a visit, particularly for its independent bookshop. This is a wide-ranging, sandy beach in a rural setting with an "away from it all" feel. Birdwatchers enjoy the dunes behind the beach, and it is part of a long stretch of walking coastline. Featuring parking right by the beach, two golf courses and cycle routes, there's plenty for everyone here. The village has become popular, reflected in the upmarket eateries and places to stay. For a peaceful walk in natural beauty, I recommend the beach to the south of the estuary. It appears out of reach from the village, but there is road access. Alternatively, climb Bracken Hill on the north side for one of the best views in Northumberland at low tide.

Runswick Bay

 Parking available

 Toilets available

 Cleveland Way

 Marine Protected Zone

 Site of Special Scientific Interest

 Dogs allowed all year round

Scan me

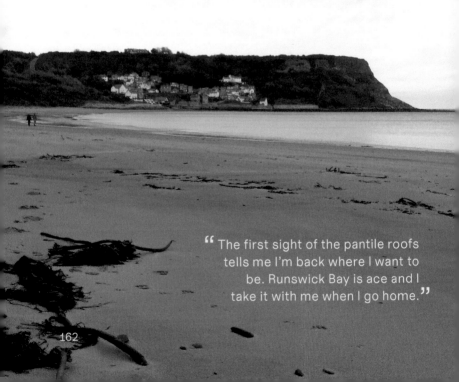

" The first sight of the pantile roofs tells me I'm back where I want to be. Runswick Bay is ace and I take it with me when I go home. "

" The beach at Runswick is very special, because it's personal to me. I have family history here. It's the peace and quiet, the beauty. It's such a stunning location, one of the best-kept secrets in England and I just love it. "

Runswick Bay, Old Norse for "safe haven", is a picturesque Yorkshire fishing village, located at the end of a valley that runs to the sea, just like Staithes further up the coast. With its sheltered bay and attractive, red-tiled roofs, it's a magnet for visitors throughout the year. A favourite attraction is a white-painted thatched cottage by the sea, which was a former coastguard's house. As well as traditional seaside activities like rockpooling and playing on the beach, this is a great place to hunt for fossils. The beautiful Cleveland Way passes above the village, offering fine views out to sea. The village is often referred to as "Runswick" and the beach is also known as "Runswick Sands". In the wider area, Whitby is just five miles away to the south, with its own thriving tourist attractions and excellent fish and chips.

Hunmanby Gap

 Parking available

 Toilets available

 Dogs allowed all year round

 Beach cleaned regularly

 Good water quality

Scan me

" As regular visitors to Filey from York, we always have a day trip down to Hunmanby Gap beach. To walk on the soft sand, with the breeze in your face and the sea out in Filey Bay puts the city behind me and frees my soul, wonderful. "

Hunmanby Gap, located just south of Filey and north of Reighton Gap, has a long sandy beach. With its easterly aspect and views to Bempton cliffs to the south, there is much to explore here. You can see a couple of intact World War II pillboxes, as well as houses perched above the soft, eroding cliffs. The long strand is a joy to walk on and the beach is always clean and sandy, as is the bathing water. Dogs are welcome here all year round. The car park is open between April and October, but there are also parking spaces on the lane throughout the year. The cafe is seasonal too. If you are walking north towards Filey, keep an eye out for the tide to avoid being cut off. This is an unspoilt environment, here to be enjoyed by all.

" As I've got older, I've started to realise how beautiful it is. I love living by the sea and especially working at Hunmanby Gap, as well. It gets prettier and prettier as the year goes on. Through summer it's absolutely gorgeous, but through winter too, when it's snowing, when it's windy, when it's raining, it's absolutely fantastic. "

Fraisthorpe

 Parking available

 Toilets available

 Dogs allowed all year round

 Beach cleaned regularly

 Good water quality

 Scan me

"Serenity. What I do like is that the waves have a serene movement to them, because it repeats, washes in, washes out. It can just take away any cares I have, by watching that."

The beach at Fraisthorpe is part of Bridlington Bay and you can see the town to the north as you walk in that direction. This is a long, sandy beach, backed by dunes, home to kitesurfers and horse riders at low tide. Access is via a narrow lane and there is parking and a cafe a short distance behind the beach. I must declare a personal historical attraction to this beach, as this is where we came as children growing up in the East Riding in the 1960s. Although there is no lifeguard service, the bathing water is clean and this is a safe swimming environment. Despite ongoing erosion along this stretch of coastline, you can still see the weathered remains of WWII pillboxes beside the dunes. This is a fine natural environment in which to unwind.

"I remember bracing swims here long ago. Wrapping my swimming trunks in my towel afterwards always meant a hot drink was coming, then off to Hornsea Pottery and home. It was a way to leave the city behind, looking back, but I just thought it was fun at the time."

Ainsdale-on-Sea

 Parking available

 Toilets available

 Ainsdale and Birkdale Hills Local Nature Reserve

 Site of Special Scientific Interest

 Dogs allowed (check locally)

 RNLI Lifeguard Cover (check locally)

 Beach cleaned regularly

 Good water quality

 Scan me

" It's just great fun to be out in the fresh air and the sunshine. It's even good fun in the rain. "

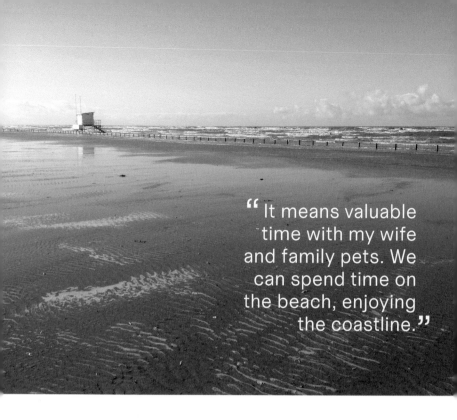

" It means valuable time with my wife and family pets. We can spend time on the beach, enjoying the coastline. "

Situated between Formby and Southport, Ainsdale beach is the only northwest England beach with a Blue Flag award for the high quality of its bathing water. The beach is regularly cleaned and there is extensive lifeguard cover. It is popular for family visits and there is a dog exclusion zone, with pets allowed elsewhere on the beach. The Ainsdale and Birkdale Hills Local Nature Reserve sits behind the dunes; this is a breeding ground for the natterjack toad. There's also The Ainsdale Discovery Centre by the beach where you can hire bikes. With water sports also high on the agenda, there's plenty for everyone at Ainsdale beach. The nearby village has restaurants and independent shops to enjoy after a bracing beach walk.

Crosby

 Parking available

 Toilets available

 Crosby Coastal Park

 Site of Special Scientific Interest

 Dogs allowed all year round

 RNLI Lifeguard Cover (check locally)

 Beach cleaned regularly

 Good water quality

 Scan me

" It's where I like to walk the dogs. I prefer it in the winter, because you get it to yourself. I'm never far from the beach, because I work on the port and drive the cranes, as well. I've got quite a decent collection of caps from here. "

This long sandy beach looks out over Crosby Channel and the busy shipping lanes in and out of Liverpool. Perhaps appropriately then, it's the location for artist Antony Gormley's Another Place, comprising a hundred cast-iron life-sized figures, each in the image of the artist. These iron men, placed at different points in the tide run, look out to sea, as many people do when standing on the beach. Not only are they barnacled and weathered, but many of the figures have bracelets and decorations, a result of human interaction. They don't appear incongruous, adding their own resonance to the question "What does the beach mean to you?" According to the artist, Another Place harnesses the ebb and flow of the tide to explore humanity's relationship with nature.

" We went to see the sculptures and I didn't realise there were so many. It shows what the sea can do over time, all the barnacles, but then everything passes eventually, doesn't it? "

171

Hoylake Red Rocks

 Parking available

 Dogs allowed all year round

 Toilets available

 RNLI Lifeguard Cover (check locally)

 Wirral Circular Trail & Wirral Coastal Walk

 Beach cleaned regularly

Hilbre Islands

 Good water quality

 Site of Special Scientific Interest

Scan me

> " This beach in particular holds a lot of memories for me. When we moved here to the first house at the end of the road here, I was seventeen. I can always remember the first morning, waking up in the dark, pulling back the curtains and looking over this incredible vista, with something of a shock and quite a pleasant surprise, to be honest. "

172

" Memories and freedom. I grew up with beach and sea
and loved the smell of the sea and the wind and the
sand. It's beautiful, it's peaceful, it's changeable and it's
unpredictable. The islands out there are beautiful, with lots
of interesting birds and small flora. At certain times of the
year, you can hear the seals singing – it's a haunting cry.
It's also a very happy place. In the summer, there is loads of
laughter. You can breathe. The air is so fresh. Just to walk
around and think 'How lucky I am to live in a place like this'. "

Also known as Hilbre Point, Red Rocks beach at Hoylake shares access
with West Kirby beach to the Red Rocks Marsh Local Nature Reserve
and its wide variety of wildlife. With views across to Hilbre Island in the
Dee Estuary and a major championship golf course nearby, it attracts
a variety of visitors. Walking is popular, along with cycling. Red Rocks
has a significant natterjack toad population. This is also a great beach
for exploring rock pools, but do be careful when the tide is coming in,
as it rises quickly. A highlight in August is the RNLI Open Day, known as
Lifeboat Day. Red Rocks hosts regular beach cleans, bathing water is up
to scratch and dogs are allowed on the beach.

Lowland
Scotland

1 – St Andrews West Sands
2 – Elie
3 – Gullane
4 – Yellowcraig
5 – North Berwick West Bay
6 – North Berwick East Bay

7 – Dunoon West Bay
8 – Fairlie
9 – Drummore
10 – Lamlash Bay
11 – Machir Bay

St Andrews West Sands

 Fife Coast Path

 Site of Special Scientific Interest

 Dogs allowed all year round

 RNLI Lifeguard Cover (check locally)

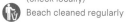 Beach cleaned regularly

 Good water quality

 Scan me

" On a day like this, it is my favourite beach in the whole UK, not just Scotland. I like the way that you can walk along the beach and always have St Andrews in the background, silhouetted against the skyline. "

" The beach is an escape for me. It is a place I go at least 4 times a week to walk my dog and clear my head. It never fails to astound me how much beauty can be found in one place and is different every time you visit. It can be the breath taking sunset or sunrise, the calmness or turmoil of the water or just a simple conversation you'll have with a stranger which will undoubtedly happen when walking on a beach in Scotland. The best feeling in the world for me is being on a beach feeling the sun on your skin and listening to the waves gently lapping at the shore, nothing else can make me feel more relaxed. "

This is the beach used in the opening sequence of "Chariots of Fire". There is plenty of space on the sand with almost two miles of beach backed by sand dunes and the world famous St Andrews golf course, known as The Home of Golf. The town is worth a visit, with a ruined cathedral on the high ground above East Sands beach. St Andrews is a university town, which also has excellent cafes and restaurants, all within an easy walk from the beach. The dunes at West Sands are part of the Firth of Tay and Eden Estuary Special Area of Conservation. As well as protecting the golf course and the town from the sea, they support many significant animal and plant species. When the sky is fused with the sea, as I found on one occasion, the horizon loses its definition. The sea lapped the shore gently as the town of St Andrews began to wake up for another day.

" Everybody loves the place. It's a dream world.
You see the water going out and you know it's
going to come in again. Life's like that too. "

Elie

 Parking available

 Toilets available

Fife Coast Path

SSSI Site of Special Scientific Interest

 Dogs allowed (check locally)

 Beach cleaned regularly

 Good water quality

Scan me

"Peace, quiet, tranquillity, lots of lovely long walks, just getting away from all the hustle and bustle of working life. It's fantastic on the beach."

" I've been coming to Elie beach for 35 years
now. I came as a small kid and I'm now bringing
my own kids. I suppose it's my favourite place in
the world. There's no other place I'd rather be. "

This long sandy beach links the former royal burghs of Elie and
Earlsferry. It features beach huts and dunes that sit behind a wide
expanse of sand at low tide. This popular swimming beach forms the
central section of a long, curved line of sand that runs from Earlsferry
round to Elie Harbour. Beach cricket is played at low tide in front of The
Ship Inn. Backed by dunes and beach huts, Elie is ideal for dinghy sailing,
pleasure boating, windsurfing and suchlike. The proximity of the village
adds variety to any visit and the wider attractions of Fife are to hand. In
addition, the beach lies on the Fife Coastal Path. I remember bright
sunshine and a blue sky greeting me one early morning in summer, yet I
also recall trudging through the snow in winter. Elie is a pleasure to visit
at any time of the year.

Gullane

 Parking available

 Toilets available

Scottish Coast Path

Aberlady Bay Local Nature Reserve

 Site of Special Scientific Interest

Dogs allowed all year round

Beach cleaned regularly

Good water quality

Scan me

> " I love to listen to the waves washing on the shore. I like to look at the sea birds and I quite like going to the pub afterwards. "

Gullane has an expansive, sandy beach, with fine views of the Firth of Forth. In the summer it is popular with families, offering kite flying, windsurfing and canoeing. In terms of natural attractions, the sea buckthorn, orange when in bloom and the extensive dune system provide a haven for small birds. There's a pleasing arc to this beach, which gradually reveals itself as you approach though the grasses and dunes. The scene might be from a children's picture book. This beach is located close to the celebrated Muirfield Golf Course. Longniddry is less than a mile away, with its shops, restaurant and train station. For walkers, the John Muir Way is a highlight at any time, but on the beach itself the rich golden colour of the sand is striking. I have visited many times, but each welcome is different in mood and temperament, such is the wonder of this beach. Once, I remember razor clam shells crunching underfoot as I walked along the strand line. On another occasion, the gentle lapping of the waves from the Firth of Forth were adequate accompaniment, so it was down to the water for a paddle. Finally, Gullane Bents is dog friendly.

Yellowcraig

 Parking available

 Toilets available

 Scottish Coastal Path

 Site of Special Scientific Interest

 Dogs allowed all year round

Beach cleaned regularly

Good water quality

Scan me

> " The beach is escape and also feeling at home. Whenever I get to the beach, on my own or with my husband or with the dogs, you calm down, you chill and all your cares disappear. You meet people on the beach. You may never see them again, but they stay in memory. It's just beautiful. I love it. "

" Freedom, the sense of quiet and still and you're able to take your thoughts down here and clear your head. A day like this is so wonderful, because this is morning breaking and as you can see from the light, it's a beautiful day, perfect for walking the dogs and blowing away the cobwebs. "

This beach is one of the jewels in the crown of East Lothian. There is a sense of drama as you approach, firstly through the band of trees then across the marram grass and dunes. The arc of the beach is the first thing to greet you. Yellowcraig is a popular family beach, with a barbecue site, nature trail and footpaths that lead through the sheltered woodlands and extensive grassland behind the beach. The beach sits within a natural cove and has spectacular views to the 1885 lighthouse on Fidra Island, the inspiration for Robert Louis Stevenson's "Treasure Island". In the nearby village of Dirleton, there is a castle with extensive gardens. To summarise, Yellowcraig has outstanding natural beauty in all directions, a magical place where the air, land and sea meet.

North Berwick West Bay

 Parking available

 Toilets available

 Scottish Coastal Path

 Site of Special Scientific Interest

Dogs allowed all year round

Beach cleaned regularly

Good water quality

 Scan me

"I just really like staying beside the sea. I'm originally from an island, so I like to be beside the sea."

" It's an endless moving picture, summer and winter.
I've lived here for ten years. I've never been any
happier than right here. This is just perfect for me. "

This is the main town beach for North Berwick and can be found near to the railway station. A wide arc of sand lines North Berwick's bays. This beach is popular with families, dog walkers and swimmers alike. The town's amenities are to hand and you can visit the lifeboat house and the Sea Bird Centre easily from here. This beach is clean, expansive and attractive, set conveniently in front of the town. I remember one summer visit. The beach was full of relaxing visitors, enjoying the blue sky, warm weather and all that North Berwick has to offer in season. Like Cromer in Norfolk, the town and the beach are in close harmony. On another visit, festival bunting lined the streets, an accordion was being played outside and seasonal shops were re-opening for the visitor season. There is a rich cultural identity here, an example being the popular East Lothian Yacht Club.

North Berwick East Bay

 Parking available

 Toilets available

 Scottish Coastal Path

 Site of Special Scientific Interest

 Dogs allowed all year round

 Beach cleaned regularly

 Good water quality

 Scan me

" I stay on the beach here. Every day it's different. There's either flat calm water, heavy seas, ships, cruise liners in the summer, dinghies, the racing for the boats. It's just a wonderful place to be. "

This is an expansive beach, also known as Milsey Bay, which affords fine views of Bass Rock and the Firth of Forth. The rocks by the beach have a pool cut into them for paddling, so it's a safe family destination. With a picturesque harbour nearby and boats to take people out from the Sea Bird Centre to Bass Rock, there are plenty of visitor attractions in this part of East Lothian. I remember once how the receding tide had filled the lido on the beach at East Bay. Groups of children paddled in the shallow sea water, warmed by the hot summer sun. Blue skies framed the enormous Bass Rock and its gannet colony offshore. One summer, I learned about the Scottish Sea Bird Centre and the boat trips to see the gannet colony.

" I think this is a really magical beach, because, as you can see, behind us is Bass Rock, which between March and October each year, is home to about 150,000 gannets, the world's largest gannet colony. To come here in the morning, just a short 25 minute train journey from Edinburgh, is something special. "

Dunoon West Bay

 Parking available

 Toilets available

 Dogs allowed (check locally)

 Beach cleaned regularly

 Good water quality

Scan me

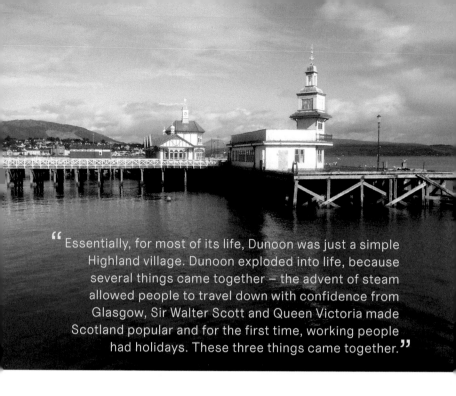

"Essentially, for most of its life, Dunoon was just a simple Highland village. Dunoon exploded into life, because several things came together – the advent of steam allowed people to travel down with confidence from Glasgow, Sir Walter Scott and Queen Victoria made Scotland popular and for the first time, working people had holidays. These three things came together."

Dunoon sits on the western side of the Firth of Clyde, with the Holy Loch to the north and Innellan to the south. West Bay beach is located to the south of the harbour and town, although there are still some houses forming a backdrop. It's a shingle beach where you can swim safely in clean bathing water. There are many scenic walks to enjoy on the Cowal Peninsula, a place to escape from the hustle and bustle of daily life. For the sightseer there is a castle, the town and a historically significant pier. This pier, originally built in 1835 to bring visitors down the Clyde from Glasgow, has been recently renovated and again welcomes the Paddle Steamer Waverley, the last seagoing paddle steamer in the world. A trip aboard is highly recommended.

"It's a great place to get outdoors every day. It's a happy place. The children use it during school term. It's a busy wee beach and you also have the cafes and the bars, so it's really good."

Fairlie

 Parking available

 Dogs allowed all year round

 Toilets available

 Beach cleaned regularly

Ayrshire Coastal Path

 Good water quality

 Site of Special Scientific Interest

Scan me

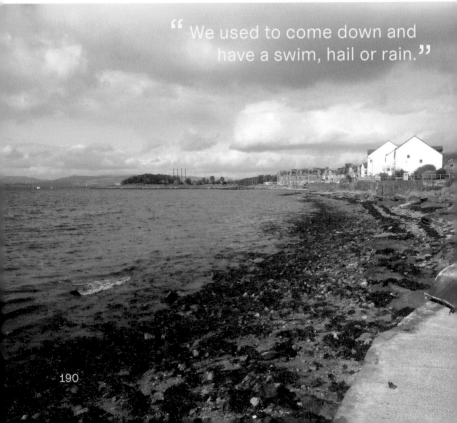

" We used to come down and have a swim, hail or rain. "

Fairlie has a long sandy beach with some shingle and rocks on the foreshore. At the southern end is a private pier where train visitors from Glasgow used to disembark. There are views to Great and Little Cumbrae Islands, as well as to the Isle of Arran. This is a favourite yachting venue and there is a slipway for dinghies. Fairlie is a quiet town nowadays, although it has a pub and a gift shop, plus a petrol station. This was not always the case. The arrival of a collection of colourful Glaswegian entrepreneurs started with John Fife in the late eighteenth century. His descendants built the famous Fife racing yachts. He was followed by the disreputable banker, Peter Peterson, who ran off with the money. The arrival of the railway in 1880 raised Fairlie's profile to that of an upmarket commuter satellite for Glasgow. Pensioners and commuters now hold sway.

" Childhood memories. My mum's aunty had a house on Ferry Road and we used to spend our holidays there as children. You could hire a rowing boat and children were playing on the beach. Years ago, the train used to come into the pier from Glasgow. It was very busy with Glasgow week. "

Drummore

 Parking available

 Toilets available

 Dogs allowed all year round

 Beach cleaned regularly

 Good water quality

 Scan me

" It's a place of escape. It's a new part of our lives, as we've just moved here. We visit here to enjoy the peace, enjoy the space and take the dog for a walk. "

"It can be so, so quiet, which is what we're seeking. We've seen a seal pop up its head and the shags. It's quite distinctive, in that it's sheltered, then you go round the corner and it's quite different, more rocky and you can see the lighthouse.**"**

Drummore is the most southerly town in Scotland, taking its name from the old Drummore Castle. The beach here faces northeast, located in the lee of the prevailing wind on the Rhins of Galloway, just above the tip, or mull. Its sheltered position makes this a popular sailing spot, featuring a slipway to help to launch dinghies and a small harbour with moorings. The origins of the harbour date back to a time in the early 1800s when there was a lime-making industry. A safe way out for the lime and in for the coal used in its production was needed. The beach is sandy and the adjacent town is friendly and welcoming, with cafes and restaurants. I recommend a visit to Galloway and to this town beach specifically.

Lamlash Bay

 Parking available

 Toilets available

 Dogs allowed all year round

 Beach cleaned regularly

 Good water quality

Scan me

" We do a lot of sailing around Scotland and the beach for us is getting a good place for access. Having a pier and a jetty here is marvellous. "

Lamlash Bay sits on the east side of Arran. From the pier there is a wonderful view across to The Holy Isle, a place of great spiritual resonance since the time of the hermit St Molaise in the sixth century. The harbour was historically more significant than Brodick Bay; for example, it sheltered King Hakon IV of Norway's boats before their defeat at the Battle of Largs in 1263. That defeat effectively ended Norwegian claims to rule the Hebrides. Nowadays it is an affluent yachting harbour and a popular visitor and tourist destination. Day trips are available to The Holy Isle, which is three kilometres long and rises to over three hundred metres at Mullach Mor. From a conservation point of view, the northern section of the bay is designated as a No Take Zone to protect marine life and fish stocks.

" For me, the beach has been part of my life since I was a child. My mother used to take us to the beach every day during the summer. We now live by the beach, we sail and it's just wonderful. We can get to places that people can't get to in cars. The boat is our lives. It's holidays. We don't do anything else. "

Machir Bay

 Parking available

 Dogs allowed all year round

Scan me

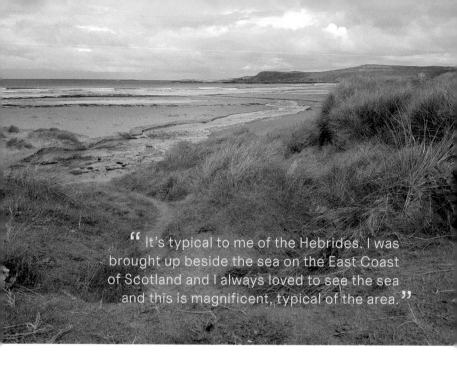

"It's typical to me of the Hebrides. I was brought up beside the sea on the East Coast of Scotland and I always loved to see the sea and this is magnificent, typical of the area."

The beach at Machir Bay, also known as Kilchoman, runs for almost two miles of exquisite soft sand, backed by dunes and machair (Gaelic for a low-lying, fertile plain), which is resplendent with wildflowers in the early summer. Located in the southwestern part of Islay, access is via a stream that runs onto the beach. Swimming is not advised here due to the strong currents. Facing west, this is also a fine place to enjoy the sunset. There is a track at the southern end of the beach leading to Kilchiaran Bay, the Iron Age fort Dun Chroisprig and Grannie's Rock. Other historical references relate to shipwrecks. One disaster occurred when two convoy ships, HMS Otranto and HMS Kashmir, collided due to navigation error in World War I.

"I would say the colours, because when we came over, there was a lovely greenness to the sea, with the sun shining on it. It's so remote and it's so quiet, a simple life and it's very enjoyable to see this."

North East and Northern Scotland

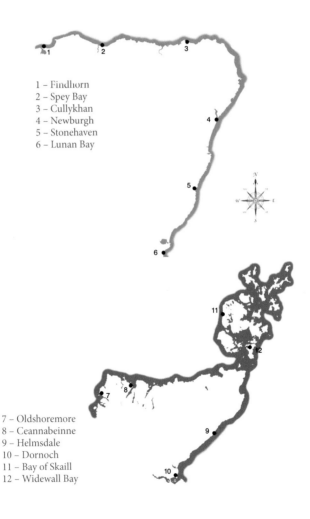

1 – Findhorn
2 – Spey Bay
3 – Cullykhan
4 – Newburgh
5 – Stonehaven
6 – Lunan Bay

7 – Oldshoremore
8 – Ceannabeinne
9 – Helmsdale
10 – Dornoch
11 – Bay of Skaill
12 – Widewall Bay

Findhorn

 Parking available

 Toilets available

 Scottish Coastal Path

 Site of Special Scientific Interest

 Dogs allowed all year round

 Good water quality

Scan me

"The beach is somewhere that soothes and comforts me, where my worries can be swept away under the waves, a place that continually inspires me."

" This particular beach is very special to me. Coming home is very heartfelt, the crunch of the pebbles under our feet, the smells of the seaweed and the broken pieces of mussel shell. It so resonates with my childhood. I love the way the water come in and out, the boats with their keels on their sides. "

The beach at Findhorn Bay in Moray sits between the pine trees of Culbin Forest to the west and Burghead Bay to the east. Grey and common seals can be found by the shore. The area was once known as Scotland's Sahara, before the forest was planted in the last century. The setting is outstanding and it is no surprise that it is part of the Culbin Sands, Forest and Findhorn Bay Site of Special Scientific Interest. Nearby Findhorn has a thriving arts scene, the Findhorn Bay Arts Festival taking place annually in September. One summer evening I visited Findhorn Bay on a high tide at the end of a day's yachting and sailing. A sand spit at the edge of the bay was still visible and the sky was a study in whites, blues and greys. The atmosphere was languid and a deep calm pervaded the waterside watchers, as they relaxed at the end of their day by the sea.

Spey Bay

 Parking available

 Dogs allowed all year round

 Toilets available

 Site of Special
Scientific Interest

 Scottish Coastal Path

 Scan me

" The iconic river Spey flows through the centre of the
reserve. On the Kingston side is an enjoyable 2-mile
circular walk which leads along the coast and back
through peaceful woodland and grassland. From the
Tugnet side you can enjoy a walk along the Speyside Way
to the viaduct and back through alder woodland. Look out
for seals, otters, deer, terns, waders and ospreys. "

Spey Bay in Moray has the largest shingle beach in Scotland, with a diverse habitat of vegetation, salt marshes and reed beds. Although there is a history of intensive salmon fishing, nowadays it is a wildlife paradise. You can often spot bottlenose dolphins, either out at sea or feeding at the mouth of the River Spey. Located just by the beach is the Scottish Dolphin Centre, whose mission is to raise awareness of whales and dolphins and efforts to protect them. The beach is a haven for breeding birds, including terns and there is a rich diversity of plants and flora here, as well as the butterflies they attract.

" I just love the beach. I love the beach in the
winter, when the sea is really wild and you get
covered in spray. I love the beach in the summer,
when you've got the dolphins coming past and
you've got the osprey there fishing and you've
got the gannets diving. I just love it all year round. "

Cullykhan

 Parking available

 Scottish Coastal Path

 Site of Special Scientific Interest

 Dogs allowed all year round

Scan me

The sandy cove at Cullykhan Bay shelters the beach from the prevailing south westerly winds, making this an idyllic location. It is overlooked by Castle Point, the site of the ancient Fort Fiddes. From the beach there is an excellent view towards Pennan and Hell's Lum, the remains of a collapsed sea cave. The Moray Firth is home to hundreds of thousands of seabirds, including puffins, fulmars, shags, kittiwakes, guillemots and razorbills, many of which can be seen here. Approached by steep steps, the stunning beach has sheer cliffs to either side. On one side you can walk through a rock tunnel to the next cove, its entrance framing a bright sky during one of my visits. Intense sunshine towards the late afternoon cast a sleepy air on proceedings and it was a pleasure on the receding tide to walk over the surface rocks and to explore the rock pools.

" I like to come to beaches to collect things. I'm an art student. This clay, it's such an expensive commodity back home and I just stumbled across it and it's completely free. People put a value on this. The commodification of natural objects. It makes me think. "

Newburgh

 Parking available

 Toilets available

 Scottish Coastal Path

 Forvie National Nature Reserve

 Site of Special Scientific Interest

 Dogs allowed all year round

Scan me

> " I've always liked the sea and I like living by the sea. I can see the sea from my house and I do find it therapeutic. After work, I walk the dog and it does clear my head. "

> **"** The beach at this moment is a part of a project where I'm collecting sand from beaches around the Northeast coast of Scotland by rolling out a 25 metre roll of Sellotape, so the sticky side is covered in sand, re-rolling it to create a cross-section of the area covered. They'll be displayed on a wall, a bit like a film reel. **"**

Located next to a golf course below the village of Newburgh, this beach is best accessed via a delightful walk along the banks of the River Ythan estuary, where it sits on the southern side, opposite the Sands of Forvie. Eider ducks and seals can be seen at close quarters, as well as terns and oystercatchers. An established dune system lies behind the beach. During a summer visit I saw seals basking in the warm, bright sunshine under blue skies. There's a fine, flat walk here through bushes and grassland to the estuary of the River Ythan, where you can look across the mouth of the river to the seals lounging on a sand spit. This side of the Ythan estuary is now protected for their benefit.

Stonehaven

 Parking available

 Toilets available

 Scottish Coastal Path

 Site of Special Scientific Interest

 Dogs allowed all year round

 Good water quality

Scan me

" There's a great peace when I look out there at the sea. Every time I come down, it's always different. It can be calm or it can be wild. Wild and wonderful, but it always looks wonderful. "

" It brings the peace and the beauty of the whole world into our lives, as we stroll along and look at that beautiful sea. We are very, very fortunate to live here. **"**

Stonehaven beach is a popular crescent of sand and shingle, accessed via a path and a boardwalk. It is a long beach that faces the North Sea, with large cliffs at either end, sheltering rock pools and inlets. The town of Stonehaven stands immediately behind. A beach pavilion on the promenade hosts the annual Stonehaven Folk Festival. New Year's Eve at Stonehaven is the time for the fireballs ceremony, with burning balls of fire, as the name suggests, making this place a great choice for Hogmanay. As well as Stonehaven's reputation for festivals, the wider area offers both history and nature, ranging from Dunnottar Castle and the Tolbooth Museum to the excellent Fowlsheugh Reserve, where you will find puffins.

Lunan Bay

 Parking available

 Toilets available

 Scottish Coastal Path

 Site of Special Scientific Interest

Dogs allowed all year round

Beach cleaned regularly

Good water quality

 Scan me

"It's a peaceful getaway, a nice, quiet place to relax and be with your own thoughts."

"It's a daily escape, a place to gather your thoughts and walk the dogs and take in the scenery and the air. What more could you ask for? It's awesome. It makes you think 'What is it? How was it all created?'"

This outstanding beach is unspoilt and beautifully positioned, well away from busy everyday lives. It features a castle, sand dunes and cliffs at one end. During my first visit, snow still lay on the beach and on the dunes, framing the arc of the bay. This is a haven of tranquillity, a throwback to simpler times, with salmon stake nets still deployed in the season. You can recharge your batteries, a real tonic. On my return during the summer, an extended spell of fine weather set the tone. Lunan Bay was bathed in bright sunshine, with blue skies above. The tide was out and the beach was being worked by a salmon netter. This activity has been taking place on Lunan Bay for hundreds of years, due to the presence of salmon rivers at either end of this wide, flat beach.

Oldshoremore

 Parking available

 Dogs allowed all year round

 Scottish Coastal Path

SSSI Site of Special Scientific Interest

 Scan me

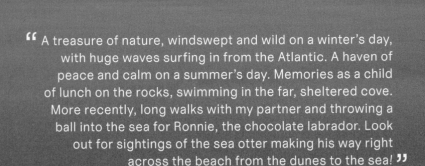

" A treasure of nature, windswept and wild on a winter's day, with huge waves surfing in from the Atlantic. A haven of peace and calm on a summer's day. Memories as a child of lunch on the rocks, swimming in the far, sheltered cove. More recently, long walks with my partner and throwing a ball into the sea for Ronnie, the chocolate labrador. Look out for sightings of the sea otter making his way right across the beach from the dunes to the sea! "

"I like to be here for the wildlife. There are otters that come down here regularly. You never know what you are going to see. I like to swim. I like to fish. If the sea is not healthy, we are not going to be healthy. It's really important."

Powdery white sand greets you as you descend through the dunes to Oldshoremore beach in Sutherland. This west-facing beach leads north. Beyond its limit is a smaller beach, which sits below Oldshorebeg. Known as Polin Beach, it is equally exquisite. The location is unspoilt and isolated. Surfers take advantage of the Atlantic swell, with its long sets of waves. Shops and restaurants are at nearby Kinlochbervie. The elemental beauty at Oldshoremore is intoxicating, with a reassuring sense of permanence. This is one of the most beautiful places in these islands.

Ceannabeinne

 Parking available

 Dogs allowed all year round

 Scottish Coastal Path

 Scan me

" The beach means to me holiday, because I am always on holiday when I am on the beach. I see the greenery, the rocks and the sea, the sand and sometimes mussels. It's calming and windy, with the noise of the sea. It's perfect for me. "

"Ceannabeinne beach is undoubtedly one of the finest beaches in Britain. Historic, proud and magnificent, a testament to the power of nature, and with no land between her shores and the North Pole! A treasure for all to admire and enjoy, locals and tourists alike."

There is history all around Ceannabeinne beach. Nearby are the remains of a monastery and a deserted village, then just over the hill is the historic eighteenth-century Rispond Harbour. Visible out to sea is Eilean Hoan, the burial island. The beach itself has pristine sand with rocky outcrops. This is a must-stop place on any tour of northern Scotland. At low tide Ceannabeinne is a candidate for the most beautiful beach in Sutherland. Visitors are met by sloping dunes, followed by mighty cliffs, both at the end and behind part of the strand. Views out to sea are stunning and the sunken setting belies the nearby road, the other side of which is a handy car park. Come to discover it for yourself – it will be worth it at any time of the year.

Helmsdale

 Parking available

 Toilets available

 Site of Special Scientific Interest

 Dogs allowed all year round

 Scan me

" It was a very important part of this community, based on the sea fishing in the great herring boom of the late eighteenth and early nineteenth centuries. The herring industry was hugely important for the community, begun as a consequence of the Highland Clearances. The coast was really a new economy, farmers turned into fishermen very quickly. "

Helmsdale was built in the early nineteenth century to resettle those dispossessed by the notorious Duke of Sutherland during the Highland Clearances. This sad period of history is marked by the Emigrants Statue, standing imposingly above the south side of the town. Further back in history there are Viking associations, due to the sheltered geography and the access inland via the River Helmsdale. Nowadays salmon fishing is still popular, but leisure craft have largely replaced the inshore fishing boats. There is a lively arts scene, including an Arts Centre and the excellent Timespan Museum. Helmsdale is well worth a visit, a popular summer event being the village's Highland Games.

" Peace and quiet and the wildlife. There seem to be more fish than a couple of years ago, so it's getting better. "

Dornoch

 Parking available

 Toilets available

 Loch Fleet

 Site of Special Scientific Interest

 Dogs allowed all year round

 Good water quality

Scan me

" The beach reminds me
of home. I'm originally
from here. It makes
me feel calm; a very
pleasant place to
spend some time. "

> " It's somewhere with a sense of freedom and being close to nature, as well as having the ability to see the world go by. I like beach-watching and seeing what other people do. "

Dornoch beach has a long expanse of golden sand. The clean bathing waters and being part of a National Nature Reserve are a winning formula. This breathtaking setting, complete with dunes and good parking, all contribute, making this a great place to visit. The eastern end of the beach is known as Burnmouth. As well as being sandy, the beach has rock pools to explore, offering fun for all the family. The nearby town of Royal Dornoch is genteel, with plenty of independent shops and eateries, as well as a world-class links golf course. I remember one summer visit to Dornoch beach. White clouds scudded by on a bright morning. Birdlife was evident along the strand, with oystercatchers and sanderlings busy at the edge of the sea. An addition to the backdrop since my previous visit was the boathouse for the East Sutherland Rescue Association (ESRA) lifeboat. ESRA is an independent service to support those at sea in the area, a fine initiative.

Bay of Skaill

 Parking available

 Dogs allowed all year

 Scan me

Site of Special Scientific Interest

 Good water quality

" The beach means clean energy and peace, a chance to see the world as it should be. "

The Bay of Skaill is a celebrated Orkney beach, not least due to the presence at its southern tip of Skara Brae, the remarkably well-preserved Neolithic village, which was inhabited 5000 years ago. The high quality of the excavations is striking, a vivid and immersive spotlight on ancient times. The rediscovered workshop is a particular highlight. The beach itself arcs pleasingly, facing the Atlantic, with its long sets of waves. As well as the heritage, this beach is a family favourite. The south side of the bay also features Hole o' Rowe, a sea arch through which waves erupt on a stormy day. One further attraction is the 1620 mansion, Skaill House.

" The Neolithic settlement of Skara Brae is situated right on the bay here. Five thousand years ago, the bay was a good bit further away. The beach is ever-changing. Every day is different. One day it's sandy, some days rocky. It's the light and the open space and the wildlife. **"**

Widewall Bay

 Parking available

 Toilets available

 Site of Special Scientific Interest

Dogs allowed all year round

  Scan me

222

In Orkney, on a beautiful day like today, it's solitude, peace, tranquillity and just beautiful scenery. Even when the weather's rougher, it's still exciting and exhilarating. The solitude is everything.

Widewall Bay is a sheltered enclave on the western side of South Ronaldsay, located by the main southerly entrance to Scapa Flow. It provides shelter for yachts, and it has a small beach. There is a heavy ancient resonance hereabouts, including the interesting Oyce of Quindry, a Neolithic site which is fully visible at low tide. This is a great birdwatching location too and there are excellent views across the bay to Hoxa and towards the picturesque village of Herston. On one occasion I visited Sands of Wright in the bay, then returned in the summer to the Oyce of Herston and the Oyce of Quindry, which can be found at the more sheltered end of the bay. Here there is another, longer strand than the one at nearby Sands of Wright beach. An oyce, pronounced "oose", is a flat inlet within an existing bay, ideal for drawing up flat-bottomed Viking boats over a thousand years ago. I strongly recommend a visit to South Ronaldsay and to this bay, with its mix of history and natural beauty.

" I've lived here for a lot of years and spent a lot of time on this beach. When my children were little, it was a fabulous place for them to play. I ride my horses along the beach. It's just incredibly beautiful. A lot of people say 'Don't you miss trees?' 'No, I don't. I do miss seeing the horizon when I am down among trees'. "

Highlands
and Islands

Clachtoll

Scan me

 Parking available

 Scottish Coastal Path

 Dogs allowed all year round

" It's my paradise for two weeks every year, but it's always with me at home or wherever else I am. It's heaven to me. "

Clachtoll beach, like Achmelvich, is located northwest of Lochinver, but further out on the Assynt Peninsula towards Point of Stoer. This is a white, powdery sand and shell beach in a rocky and rugged setting, with a feature called the Split Rock. Although it is unspoilt, there is a convenient static caravan park nearby. The whole Assynt Peninsula is a tonic, giving a wonderful sense of space and detachment away from the hurly burly of modern life. There's also a discreet, family-friendly campsite and holiday cottage nestled behind the dunes, if you are staying overnight. On one occasion, my arrival coincided with the Scottish schools' summer holidays. A piper played in the dunes at the end of the day. It was a moving experience.

" Exploration, with the rock pools and what you can find in them, fish and crabs, finding something different that you've not seen before. Then the expanse of the sea and swimming in it. Just having fun with your family. "

" I came up here thirty years ago and fell in love with it. How
could you not? It's pure white sand, beautiful blue water.
You could be in the Caribbean. Kids have brilliant fun on this
beach. My five grandchildren were all up here at Easter and
they were all playing here, building sandcastles. "

Gairloch

 Parking available

 Toilets available

 Scottish Coastal Path

 Dogs allowed all year round

Scan me

> " I like swimming in the sea and I go in all year round. I go with a bunch of mad people and what I love about it is the shared madness. "

" It takes us back. From tiny babies, we've both been taken to the beach on holiday. With our own children and grandchildren, we just love to feel that feeling we had as children and watch them having great fun. We can think 'Wow, we've got grandchildren now to watch playing on the beach'. **"**

There is more than one beach on the edge of Loch Gairloch in Wester Ross. You have a choice between the expansive Big Sand beach, facing south, the beach at Gairloch itself, just in front of the west-facing golf course and further beaches at Red Point, round to the south of the bay. The sea loch also gives access to the village and yachting haven of Badachro, a sheltered area of creeks and woods. In short, this is a varied natural environment, with all the modern conveniences that you'll need in Gairloch itself. On one occasion I explored its southern edge, settling at beautiful Red Point beach. I approached via high dunes. Round stones, sculpted and smoothed by the sea, are scattered at the back of the beach. The tide was out and the sea was tranquil. There are fine views here across to the Black Cuillins on Skye, south to Loch Torridon and even across the Minch to the Isle of Harris on a clear day. On another fine weather day, Big Sand beach was the setting for my visit to Gairloch. This is the most expansive of the beaches around the bay, with tall dunes that sit behind the beach. Out to sea, whales and dolphins can be spotted in the wide bay as you look across to Badachro. This is a fine beach for walking among myriad elemental stimuli.

Plockton

 Parking available

 Scottish Coastal Path

 Dogs allowed all year round

 Scan me

230

> **"** We come down every single year, because our sister lives here. It's the first beach in Plockton that we swam on and it's just gorgeous, the most peaceful beach in the area. We beachcomb and we find interesting things every time we go. **"**

The village of Plockton is one of the tourist magnets in the Highlands, an attractive and sheltered haven for passing yachts. Known as "The Jewel of the Highlands", the village has an upmarket feel during the summer season. Fishing and crofting have long since been displaced by Plockton's popularity as a yachting anchorage and a highlight of the season is the two-week sailing regatta. Other popular water sports include kayaking and rowing. The beach here is known as Coral Beach and can be found a mile or so outside the village, an oasis of tranquillity. It is well worth the walk to find such a peaceful strand, with its surface made of dried, calcified seaweed, known as maerl. The nature here is pristine.

> **"** This beach is really special, but it reminds me of all the lovely beaches and beachcombing of my childhood. We like the low tide and finding what's left over after the tide has gone out, shells, bits of string, odd little things that get washed up in the tide. We keep a little collection at home. **"**

Glenelg

 Parking available

 Toilets available

 Scottish Coastal Path

 Dogs allowed all year round

 Beach cleaned regularly

Good water quality

 Scan me

"A quiet corner of the Highlands, not as busy as it used to be, thank goodness."

The stunning setting for the hamlet of Glenelg includes a wide variety of attractions, despite its isolated location. You usually approach via a single-track road which joins the main A87 at the foot of Glen Shiel and the head of Loch Duich. Alternatively, you can cross Kyle Rhea from Skye via the Glenelg ferry to the north of Glenelg, a historical reference to the original main route "over the sea to Skye". Celebrated traveller Samuel Johnson and his faithful friend James Boswell popularised the village, but the area is steeped in history for other reasons. One example is the tradition of Highland cattle from Skye swimming, guided by a rowing boat, ashore on route to market. Also there is the ruined yet imposing Bernera Barracks, one of the four main English forts established following the Jacobite uprising. Other historical attractions are the well-preserved Glenelg brochs, ancient circular defensive towers. These examples are located by Gleann Beag, a short distance south of Glenelg. This is a wonderful place to visit, steeped in history and natural beauty.

" It's a link back to the past for me, strangely. My surname is Scottish, by descent. I feel a very close link to the islands. There are also all those traditions based on boundaries, between land and water, such as liminal burial grounds. "

Camusdarach

 Parking available

 Toilets available

 Scottish Coastal Path

 Dogs allowed all year round

Scan me

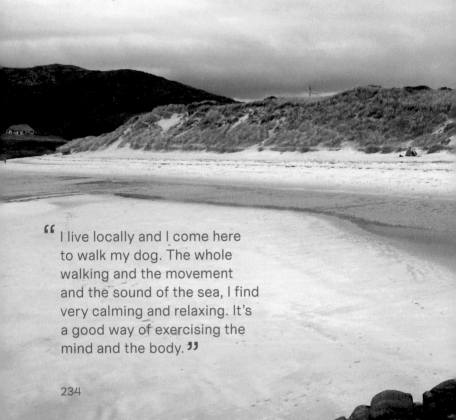

" I live locally and I come here
to walk my dog. The whole
walking and the movement
and the sound of the sea, I find
very calming and relaxing. It's
a good way of exercising the
mind and the body. "

234

"This place is very special to me and my family. It just represents freedom. Children can just be children. They have a lot of space, they run around, there is nobody to tell them to be quiet. They love to go in the sea. It's a slice of heaven for us."

This is a candidate for the most beautiful beach in Scotland. Chosen as a location for many films, including "Highlander" with Sean Connery and Christopher Lambert, one of the Harry Potter films and the wonderful "Local Hero", the beach enjoys spectacular views across to Eigg and Rum from its pristine shoreline. The approach is over dunes. The sand is powder fine and the natural beauty can stop any visitor in their tracks. It's safe to swim from the beach and the peace and quiet is soothing. Located on the Road to the Isles, both the Sands of Morar and Arisaig are reasonably near. There is a campsite with stunning views behind the beach.

Ardnamurchan Point

 Parking available

 Toilets available

 Scottish Coastal Path

 Site of Special Scientific Interest

 Dogs allowed all year round

 Scan me

"The beach means everything to me. I'm very much a sea person and I love being by the coast. I think it's the most refreshing, happy, healthy that I ever am. I just think it's the best thing in the world."

❝Ardnamurchan Point is such a special spot – not only the most Westerly point on the British Mainland, but a great location to see out to Coll, Tiree and the Small Isles; the islands feel so close. If you are really lucky in the summer months, basking sharks can be seen off the point.❞

Located seven miles south of the Small Isle of Muck, Ardnamurchan Point is the most westerly point in mainland Britain. On arrival, the most striking sight is the lighthouse that Alan Stevenson built in 1849. Standing eight metres high, there is an inscription on the wall inside, penned by fellow family member Robert Louis Stevenson, as follows:

> "For love of lovely words, and for the sake
> Of those, my kinsmen and my countrymen,
> Who early and late in the windy ocean toiled
> To plant a star for seamen, where was then
> The surfy haunts of seals and cormorants:
> I, on the lintel of this cot inscribe
> The name of a strong tower."

As you can imagine, this is an isolated spot, forming the southern edge of Sanna Bay and approached by a long single-track road. The beach is pristine and unspoilt, with the view extending as far north as Skye. It's a great getaway location, a fine place to regain or confirm perspective.

Ganavan Sands

 Parking available

 Toilets available

 Scottish Coastal Path

 Dogs allowed all year round

Scan me

"Take me to a beach and even if I'm working, I'm on holiday."

Ganavan Sands is located a mile or so north of Oban, looking across the bottom of Loch Linnhe to the Sound of Mull. It's a picturesque, sandy Blue Flag beach and is easily accessed from the town. Oban is the gateway to Mull and has become a tourist destination, featuring the imposing McCaig's Tower that sits above the town and Dunollie Castle, which stands on a rocky ridge overlooking the sea. It also bills itself as "the Seafood Capital of the Highlands". With views across to the hills of Mull, as well as to Lismore and mainland Morven behind, this is an excellent getaway beach for the people of Oban. There is a fine coast walk to the north, where peace and tranquillity can be found on soft grassy knolls. On one visit I remember a fine palette of greys, whites, blacks and blues, with the sea melding into the sky.

" The beach to me is magical. As soon as you step onto the beach, it's like another world. You look round it, you see so many different things and you meet different people all the time, different nationalities, out with their dogs, out with their children and you can just tell instantly that they all love it. "

Claigan Coral Beach

  Site of Special Scientific Interest

Dogs allowed all year round

Scan me

> " Just take a look at it. It's absolutely breathtaking, isn't it? You've got beautiful white sand, beautiful aqua water. It is absolutely stunning. "

> " I always find beaches to be comforting. They are always places to go to be with your family or just by yourself, to be surrounded by the beautiful nature. "

You follow the road north from Dunvegan on Skye to find this beach. Parking at Claigan, you will find a lane that leads to the beach. Comprising dried, calcified maerl, a local seaweed, Coral Beach is next to Loch Dunvegan, a short walk past the sandy beach at Camas Bàn, where you pass through a gap in the wall. The route is straightforward and well signposted. The sea is translucent and there is a Caribbean feel to the shoreline, topped off by the outstanding views across the loch which take in the islands of Lampay and Isay. In any weather Claigan Coral Beach makes a case for inclusion in the "best beaches..." listings. On one early morning visit it was showcased in the middle of a breathtaking vista under tranquil blue skies, the maerl beach and turquoise sea tempting me in for a swim or a paddle. I like to climb the hill behind the beach and look out towards South Harris in the Western Isles, wondering who has passed this way through millennia.

Talisker

 Dogs allowed all year round

Scan me

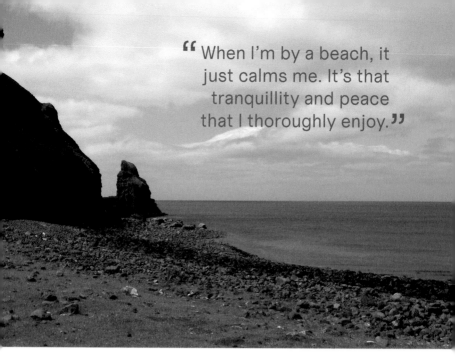

> **"** When I'm by a beach, it just calms me. It's that tranquillity and peace that I thoroughly enjoy. **"**

The beach at Talisker Bay is best seen at low tide, with its mix of stones and sand. A sharp-sided sea stack guards one end of the bay and there is a waterfall on the vertical cliffs at the other side. This is a highly charged natural setting, sitting at the foot of the Cuillin Hills on Skye. A highlight is the sunset, due to the atmospheric rocks and its westerly aspect. The walk to the beach from Talisker House is one of the most beautiful approaches you could imagine, particularly in high summer, as was the case on one of my visits. The glen draws you down to the sea and a sense of anticipation is unavoidable. The impact on arrival is ancient, volcanic and elemental. The beach can often showcase black sand as a result, but on this occasion, it was mixed with grey. It feels as if you are in a cauldron of dynamic creation.

> **"** To me, the beach is the epitome of the island, roaring seas and rocks. It doesn't have to be sand to be a beach to me. I love this one particularly, because it is so remote, the colours, the birds, the cliffs. It's very remote. **"**

Calgary Bay

 Parking available

 Toilets available

 Site of Special Scientific Interest

 Dogs allowed all year round

 Scan me

" This is her idea of heaven. And I like to stroll here with her, searching for interesting flotsam and jetsam, my head full of nothing very much at all. Even on the cold, wild and windy days, there is peace here. "

" There is something very exhilarating when a storm is raging and the wild waves roar as they tumble up the beach. Something very peaceful when the sea is still and calm and quiet with barely a wave and no-one else around. And in the height of summer, when the tide is out and the sands are dotted with family groups all enjoying a day on the beach, there is still room for me to walk and enjoy being there too. If you are lucky you might see an otter on the shore, or a white-tailed eagle soaring high above you, or a pod of dolphins breaching in the bay. **"**

Located in the northwest corner of Mull, Calgary Bay is one of the finest beaches in Scotland. The dunes are home to varied flora and fauna. The Friends of Calgary Bay provide guidance and information on such topics as wild camping and how to protect the sensitive natural balance of the beach environment, whilst welcoming the many visitors that flock here. This is one of the few beaches on Mull that are backed by shell sand dunes and machair. To one side of the beach and above is the "Art in Nature" initiative, a wooded nature trail that features various art installations, well worth a visit.

Bay at the Back of the Ocean

Dogs allowed all year round

Scan me

" As long as I can remember, I've always been living near the beach. There's a sense of freedom and quiet. You think things over, or you don't think of anything at all. "

" For me the Bay at the Back of the Ocean represents a place
to stop and consider life's journey, as America is the next
stop. I think of all the stones being tumbled over and over
in all their myriad colours and combinations. I think of the
shipwreck there in the late 1800s and what the weather
must have been like, waves breaking high over the rocks.
I always look for the jet from the spouting cave, nature's
power being expressed in a very dramatic way. The golf
course passing over the area and the tracks over the machair
make me think of different people and the many times I
have been here. I think of my parents with a picnic and my
brothers and I seeing who could jump furthest out off the
edge of the sand dunes at the edge of the beach. So the
beach means beauty, finding unexpected treasures amongst
its stones, family holidays every summer and being at the
edge, where weather can be experienced at its rawest. "

From the Gaelic Camas Cùil an t-Saimh, the bay has this name due to the clear
run west, over the Atlantic Ocean to Canada. The beach is one of several on
Iona, a small island to the west of Mull, connected by a ferry. The island has an
iconic abbey, reputedly where St Columba landed from Ireland on his Christian
mission. Columba's success in spreading Christianity onto the Scottish mainland
made Iona a culturally significant place within the Gaelic kingdom of Dal Riata,
which once dominated western Scotland and the West Highlands. The former
Labour leader, John Smith, is also buried here. As you approach the beach over
the hill, the machair ends and a bank of shingle fringes the white beach sand. It's
a magical vista that draws you down to this beautiful place.

Tolsta

 Parking available

 Dogs allowed all year round

Toilets available

 Good water quality

Scan me

" I just love coming down here to watch the sea, the waves, the birds, just freedom and taking my dog for walks. "

" Freedom. You come down here to relax and get away
from it all. In the summer people come from all over
the world, so it's good to meet different people then,
but it's also good to get away from everyday life. **"**

Tolsta is a relatively large Hebridean village which is quite remote,
located fourteen miles north of Stornoway on the Isle of Lewis.
Facing east across The Minch towards the Scottish mainland, the main
beach is reasonably sheltered and popular with surfers. It is the largest
beach on Lewis and is truly spectacular. There are invigorating coastal
walks here and the neighbouring Garry beach is exquisite, a real jewel.
I would say that these two beaches are among the most spectacular on
my travels so far. Whilst most fashionable UK beaches tend to face west,
here is evidence of stunning east-facing beauty. You can head south from
Tolsta Head down to Tràigh Mhòr, meaning big beach, or north, all the
way up to Port of Ness.

Huisinis

 Parking available

 Dogs allowed all year round

 Toilets available

 Good water quality

SSSI Site of Special Scientific Interest

 Scan me

> "The beach to me is total therapy. I can enjoy the sound of the waves, the sky, the sun, the wind and I can just relax."

If you want stunning beauty in an isolated setting, this could be the place for you. Huisinis beach can be found at the end of a long single-track road in the southwest of North Harris. It is an area of outstanding natural beauty, with excellent sea trout and salmon fishing. On the way to the beach, you pass Amhuinnsuidhe Castle with cannons pointing seaward and there are just a few houses by the beach itself. Across the isthmus is the island of Scarp, the site of an experimental rocket postal service. The beach is no disappointment, with white sand and backed by cropped grass. If you stroll over the back of the hill, more visual splendours await, with a glimpse of St Kilda on the horizon, if you are lucky.

"It was only later in life that I came to appreciate the beach. As you get older, you appreciate the world around you and the scenery. You couldn't have a better place to be than on the beach."

Seilebost

 Parking available

 Good water quality

SSSI Site of Special Scientific Interest

 Dogs allowed all year round

Scan me

" There is nothing in this world to compare with a walk on Seilebost Beach on the Isle of Harris to invigorate the soul. **"**

" Here, the beach is so closely linked with the land use of this coastal strip, what we call machair and the ecology of this area too. The beautiful sand that we see here is actually 80 to 90 percent crushed shells, which is very rich in calcium. With the climate that we have here, huge winter storms blow a lot of this onto the machair and that's what starts to form this incredibly rich coastal grassland. **"**

Seilebost beach sits at the southern edge of Luskentyre Bay, sharing the idyllic location with Luskentyre beach, which in turn sits on the northern edge. Both beaches are part of the National Scenic Area of South Lewis, Harris and North Uist. This beach is easily accessed from the adjacent main road. A feature of Seilebost is the chance to witness magnificent sunsets. Whale-watching trips run from here and there is just a smattering of houses and crofts. The machair habitat behind the beach, a grassy area enriched by the calcified seaweed or maerl, blown in from the sea, produces magnificent displays of wildflowers during the early summer. This is helped by the presence of Highland Cattle, initially brought in for commercial reasons to replace the indigenous crofters, who were displaced to the east coast.

Borve

 Parking available

 Good water quality

Scan me

 Dogs allowed all year round

> **"** When I look out onto the sea, when I'm standing on the beach, particularly in the summer, it reminds me of my Dad going past in his fishing boat and the bright, long summer days. **"**

This is one beach of many that run down the west coast of South Harris. Borve beach is deeper and less wide than neighbouring Scaristavore and Scarista beyond. A spectacular panorama unfolds as you look out from the beach towards the sea. The beach faces west and is sandy, unspoilt and in harmony with the machair behind, which itself becomes a panoply of wild flowers in high summer. For a wider perspective, climb up past Macleod's Stone, sitting at the end of Tràigh Iar, which is further along between Borve and Horgabost beaches; there's a fine beach and sea view to enjoy. This is a top location for anyone with an adventurous nature.

> **"** It doesn't matter what the question is, the answer is the beach! A place of beauty, transient light, energy, excitement, reflection and possibilities. This boundary between the elements, the ever-changing fringe, where the otters run, the porpoises hunt the waves and the eagle soars above. The sound of the surf on Borve beach calls me to return to this place, a tonic to the body and the soul. It uplifts the human in us all and reminds me to just be. **"**

Howmore

 Parking available

 Toilets available

 Site of Special Scientific Interest

Dogs allowed all year round

Good water quality

Scan me

" The most incredible sunsets, peace and tranquillity, nothing more to add. "

" Howmore beach reminds me of my childhood many years ago, walking and playing on this beautiful beach that stretches for miles, then walking to church in Bornish on Sundays. I remember crofters gathering seaweed for their crops, Tom cutting tangles while his dogs played on the beach, looking out to sea to our nearest neighbours, Nova Scotia and Canada. "

This beach on the west side of South Uist has the familiar machair, with summer wildflowers behind, which is designated as the South Uist Machair Special Area of Conservation. Visitors will be struck by the thatched crofts that sit behind the beach. I first visited the bottom section, below the village of Howmore. This part of the beach is known as Stoneybridge, with the road behind close to the sea and often awash with storm debris. There's a collection of ruined churches and chapels, giving a sense of travelling back in time and exuding a rather foreboding sensation. The beach stretches out to the north, as far as Ardivachar Point (Gaelic, Rubha Aird na Mhachair). On another occasion I returned to Howmore itself, walking past the chapel, down to the white, sandy beach, with its river running to the sea and its sheltering dunes. This beach is stunningly beautiful, with an unspoilt backdrop and a sense of timelessness. The area has been the site of religious settlements and churches for many centuries, but nature is the star here, in all its glory.

Wales

1 – Whitesands Bay
2 – Little Haven
3 – Broad Haven South
4 – Port Eynon

5 – Church Bay
6 – Porth Oer
7 – Pwllheli
8 – Morfa Bychan –
    Black Rock Sands
9 – Barmouth

Whitesands Bay

 Parking available

 Toilets available

 Pembrokeshire Coast Path

 Dogs allowed (check locally)

 RNLI Lifeguard Cover (check locally)

 Good water quality

Scan me

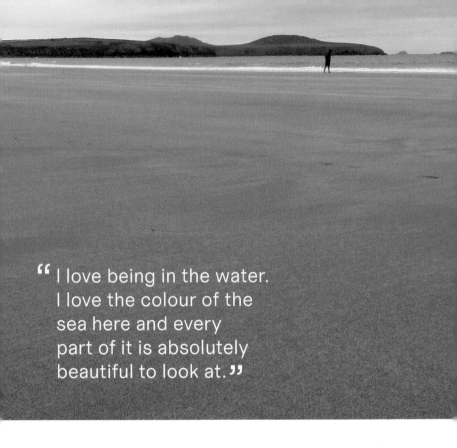

" I love being in the water. I love the colour of the sea here and every part of it is absolutely beautiful to look at. "

The mile long, south-facing beach at Whitesands Bay is a magnet for day trippers, surfers and water sports enthusiasts. There are views across to South Bishop lighthouse and Ramsey Island. Despite its popularity, there is plenty of room for everyone. The beach is the proud holder of a European Blue Flag and has St David's at the end of its headland. With the St David's golf course, a hotel and beach shop to hand, most people will be catered for. On one occasion I remember the gentle, rolling nature of the waves as they came ashore on an ebb tide. The flat, sandy beach glistened, recently washed by the receding sea.

"I come here for the fishing and the birds. Not too many other people come here. It's about the natural world for me here and I love it."

Little Haven

 Parking available

 Dogs allowed all year round

 Toilets available

Pembrokeshire Coast Path

 Scan me

"The beach means a huge amount to me. I've always sought it out and I realise that it's the sea that pulls me to the beach. I swim before eight in the morning, which is tremendous. I can't imagine life without being able to get to a beach."

❝ We love the beach at Little Haven, due to the idyllic peacefulness of its picture postcard surroundings. There are several good quality pubs and it's a lovely place to kick back and relax, while listening to the waves crashing against the surrounding cliffs. A short walk along the coastal path brings you to the Settlands, a wide bay, and to St Brides Haven, which is a real hidden treasure, where those 'in the know' can sometimes be found swimming in the sea. ❞

Little Haven and Great Haven beaches are conjoined at low tide, but they each have a different ambience. Little Haven is the strand for the upmarket village which sits at the upper reaches of its small shingle beach. Holiday cottages and dive boats proliferate, making this an ideal location for water sports and other adrenalin-fuelled activities. The slipway enables the easy launching of dinghies and other craft. A small adjacent beach, accessed via a steep path, is known as "The Sheep Wash" and is a popular location for sea swimming. Other highlights are the rock pools and the wonders they contain.

Broad Haven South

 Parking available

 Toilets available

 Pembrokeshire Coast Path

 Site of Special Scientific Interest

 National Trust

 Dogs allowed all year round

 Beach cleaned regularly

Scan me

" I return regularly to this beach. It is so natural and unspoilt. The walk round to Barafundle Bay is second to none. Look out for choughs on the grassy clifftops. "

" I suppose at this time of the morning it's an area of seclusion, a time to think. With the sea near the beach, with things constantly moving and changing, there's always something happening, something to look at. There's a beautiful sea stack out in the sea. It's a glorious morning with glorious weather. **"**

Broad Haven South beach sits a mile southeast of Bosherston village. The beautiful, golden beach is edged by grey limestone cliffs and pointed sea stacks. The sand is soft and child friendly. Sitting between Stackpole and St Govan's headlands in Pembrokeshire, the main sea stack is known as Church Rock. Behind the beach is a dune system, interspersed with marram grass, a haven for wildlife. In the eighteenth century, Baron Cawder dammed tidal creeks which used to run inland from Broad Haven. A large freshwater lake system was created, the Bosherston Lily Ponds. During one early summer visit the ponds were covered in white lilies and I was fortunate to catch a glimpse of an otter. The dunes are developing and the seasonal changes in the beach's appearance, flat in summer, gouged and channelled during winter storms, are part of the elemental appeal here. On the western side there are caves and water springs to explore, while to the east you'll find a system of smaller caves in the low cliffs.

Port Eynon

 Parking available

 Toilets available

 Wales Coast Path

 Dogs allowed (check locally)

 RNLI Lifeguard Cover (check locally)

 Beach cleaned regularly

 Scan me

"Today it's peace and quiet, a chance to reflect, a place to meditate. It's also a place I remember as a child, but never appreciated its beauty until I went away."

" I love beaches. I come to them whenever I can. I like walking on the beach, running on the beach, but swimming in the sea is a central part of it. "

One of the Gower Peninsula's most popular beaches, Port Eynon is safe for swimming and is a magnet for water sports enthusiasts. Boating, windsurfing and kitesurfing are enjoyed here. The beach is backed by dunes and shrubs and there are campsites and accommodation nearby. Port Eynon is a happy place for families, with a stunning landscape and an idyllic village nearby. There is a magnificent arc to the beach, which seems to frame the bay, particularly on an ebb tide. On one occasion it was a balmy, hot afternoon, with the horizon out of focus, due to the heat haze. This created an other-worldly atmosphere, dream-like in the warmth, accompanied by the rhythm of the waves. There is a fine seven-mile walk along the coast from here to Rhossili.

Church Bay

 Parking available

 Toilets available

 Anglesey Coastal Path

 Site of Special Scientific Interest

 Dogs allowed all year round

 RNLI Lifeguard Cover (check locally)

 Beach cleaned regularly

Good water quality

 Scan me

" The beach means a total sense of relaxation, solitude and realising that the world is such a beautiful place. **"**

It is a short walk from the village of Rhydwyn down a steep path to a beautiful bay which harbours this fine little beach, made up of rocks, pebbles and sand. The Ynys Môn (Anglesey) Coast Path follows the steep cliffs behind the beach, and and there is a handy car park. This is a Blue Flag beach, which is cleaned regularly and therefore ideal for paddling or swimming. Sailing and fishing are also popular at Church Bay. The sunset is a highlight here, which I was lucky enough to witness during one visit. At such a time, the horizon seems far away and enticing.

" It's where man meets nature. It makes you appreciate your place in the world. It's vibrant, life at its best. "

Porth Oer

 Parking available

 Toilets available

 Llyn Coastal Path

 National Trust

 Dogs allowed all year round

 Scan me

" The beach means peace and quiet, especially early in the morning, the best time to be here. As a child, I remember the squeaky sand, walking on the beach. "

Located on the north coast of the Llŷn peninsula, Porth Oer beach is popular with surfers and body boarders, due to the deep swells that arrive here. Nearby Mynydd Carreg makes a fine lookout point for nature lovers. The views from the beach are outstanding and there are footpaths through the dunes to explore, enjoying the wildlife as you go. The beach is also known as Whistling Sands due to the sound made by the beach when you walk along it. With a seasonal cafe and a picnic site, plus nearby National Trust parking, this is a great place to explore.

" Coming out here helps you commune with nature and hear things. We slept here in the dunes last night. We thought it would be all about looking at the stars and the waves, but it was really noisy from all the animals we heard, including the mysterious terns. **"**

Pwllheli

 Parking available

 Toilets available

 Llyn Coastal Path

 Dogs allowed (check locally)

 Beach cleaned regularly

 Good water quality

Scan me

" It's my escape, really. I enjoy the privacy
and I enjoy the fishing, usually for bass. "

Pwllheli has two Blue Flag beaches, each with excellent bathing water quality. Being part of a Special Area of Conservation, there is the chance to see wildflowers in the dunes and dolphins out in Cardigan Bay. The shingle South Beach stretches from Gimblet Rock along the promenade towards Llanbedrog. Glan-y-Mor beach is located at the back of the marina; it is sandy and runs for three miles to the Pen-yChain headland. During the summer, Pwllheli is very popular with visitors. The town is a magnet for shoppers and those looking for a bite to eat. Keep an eye on the tide, as the pull is strong during the middle of the tide run and can catch people out.

" We come to Pwllheli each year for our holidays.
It's a great town and a great base to explore
the beautiful Llŷn peninsula. Just perfect. "

Morfa Bychan – Black Rock Sands

 Parking available

 Toilets available

 Wales Coast Path

 Dogs allowed all year round

 Scan me

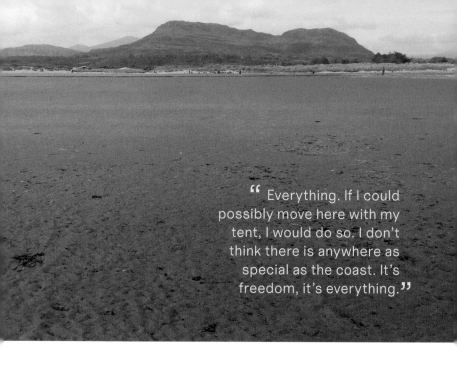

"Everything. If I could possibly move here with my tent, I would do so. I don't think there is anywhere as special as the coast. It's freedom, it's everything."

This beach sits at the northern edge of the mouth of Tremadog Bay, so the intertidal nature makes it a haven for wading birds. There is excellent walking in the area. The beach is flat, expansive and sandy, backed by an atmospheric ring of hills. Both boating and bird watching are popular here, as well as windsurfing and kitesurfing in the bay. The slipway makes boating and sailing straightforward. Visitors can park on the beach and this is a popular picnic spot. The spectacular countryside and the mountains of Eryri (Snowdonia) are visible from the beach and Porthmadog is a couple of miles away for a change of scene.

"It means employment for a lot of people. There's usually a crew of ten of us on the beach, mainly students, who join us in the summer. Every car that comes onto the beach, we give them a pass."

Barmouth

 Parking available

 Toilets available

 Wales Coast Path

 Dogs allowed (check locally)

 Beach cleaned regularly

 Good water quality

 Scan me

" I've been visiting Barmouth since I was a child, every summer. I look forward to returning to familiar places, with so many memories of happy times. Three cheers for Barmouth. "

" I've spent quite a lot of time on this beach through the years, even now, getting towards being middle-aged, enjoying the beach, enjoying the scenery. It's beautiful scenery in a wonderful part of the world. "

Looking out to Cardigan Bay in the Eryri (Snowdonia) National Park, Barmouth has a sandy beach that is popular with families. The promenade behind the beach carries a land train and there are amusements and other entertainment nearby. Water sports enthusiasts are attracted here so there is plenty for everyone at Barmouth. Sea swimming has become popular in recent years and the town supports many organised swimming events. Every kind of entertainment is available on this beach, from donkey rides to swing boats. Why not try a trip around the estuary in a pleasure boat? If you want to explore further, Eryri's wonderful hills are close by.